Prophesying for a Release of Faith

Bruce D. Reekie

Sovereign World

Sovereign World Ltd
PO Box 777
Tonbridge
Kent TN11 9XT
England

All quotations are from the New King James Bible unless otherwise stated.

NASB – The New American Standard Bible © Copyright The Lockman Foundation, 1960, 1962, 1963, 1968, 1971, 1972, 1973, 1975, 1977. La Habra, California.

TLB – The Living Bible © Copyright 1971 Tyndale House Publishers, Wheaton, Illinois 60187, USA.

Amplified – The Amplified Bible. Old Testament copyright © 1965, 1987 by the Zondervan Corporation. The Amplified New Testament copyright © 1957, 1987 by the Lockman Foundation. Used by permission.

ISBN 1 85240 093 5

Typeset by CRB (Drayton) Typesetting Services, Drayton, Norwich
Printed in England by Clays Ltd, St Ives plc.

Contents

Foreword

All around the world, God, by His Spirit, is bringing a restoration of the prophetic ministry. Even though the Pentecostal church has, by tradition, been open to the gift of prophecy, it has in the main experienced a very low level of it and not embraced the mantle of the Prophet.

This book, *Prophesying for a Release of Faith*, is like an appetiser before the meal, designed to stir up the taste buds so that the full enjoyment of the main meal can be had. Paul's admonition to the Church is, *'Covet to prophesy,'* and also, *'You all may prophesy one by one.'* He speaks of the edifying nature of prophecy and encourages us to *'seek that ye may excel to the edifying of the Church.'*

A fresh wind of the Spirit is blowing, seeking to activate the saints in the gifts of the Spirit and making way for a greater manifestation of God's presence. Gifts without His presence we have had, leaving people dry of heart. A great cry has ascended from the hearts of God's people like evaporating water, but God is sending it back to the Church as showers of rain. Zechariah 10:1 says: *'Ask ye of the Lord rain in the time of the latter rain; so the Lord shall make bright clouds, and give them showers of rain, to every one grass in the field.'*

This book will stir you up to seek God for revival. May He raise up many prophets and release many of the saints into the gifts of the Spirit. I am of the opinion that God is looking for a Prophetic Church in these great days of harvest. Numbers 12:29: *'Would God that all the Lord's people were prophets and that the Lord would put his Spirit upon them.'*

Rev. Arden Burrell
Senior Minister
Dubbo Assembly of God
New South Wales
Australia

Chapter 1

Prophesying a New Move Forward

The Body of Messiah is standing in the beginnings of a new movement of God's Spirit. The greatest revival and outpouring of the Spirit that the world has ever seen is in the earth today. It will not fail or decrease, but overcome and increase until it fills every city and nation with the manifest glory of God.

The Lord God is breathing life into His Church. He is raising her to a consciousness of the dominion of the Son of God over demons, disease and death! From the four corners of the earth God is calling together a *people*, whom He is integrating into a *body*, which He is training and equipping to function as a mighty *army*!

Once again, the people of God are standing on the banks of the Jordan, gazing across to the 'Promised Land'. Once again, 'Joshua' is commanding the 'officers' of the people to pass through the camp and say to the people, *'Prepare provisions for yourselves, for within three days you will cross over this Jordan, to go in and possess the land which the LORD your God is giving you to possess'* (Joshua 1:10, 11)

The Church stands on the threshold of taking entire cities and nations for the kingdom of God. The LORD Jesus, to whom the inheritance of the nations rightfully belongs, recognizes better than anyone else the urgency of the hour, and accordingly, He is commanding His shepherds to prepare themselves and their flocks for a new move forward.

Sounding the Advance

How will the Church enter into and conclusively possess the promised land of spiritual authority over nations? ***Through the strong prophetic utterances of the Holy Spirit!***

> '*And the* LORD *spoke to Moses, saying: "Make two silver trumpets for yourself; you shall make them of hammered work; you shall use them for calling the assembly and for directing the movement of the camps."*' (Numbers 10:1, 2)

Isaiah 58:1 identifies the 'trumpet' as the voice of the Prophetic Word: '*Cry aloud, spare not; lift up your voice like a trumpet...*' Thus, the Prophetic Word is the '*silver trumpet*' with which God calls His people together in preparation for a new move forward.

The Prophetic Word not only signals that it is time to move forward; it also *directs* the movement of the camps. The Prophetic Word not only inspires to action; it also brings divine order and a sense of direction.

The Prophetic Word says, 'Now is the time, prepare to move,' and moreover, '*This is the way, walk in it; do not turn to the right or the left.*'

The Prophetic Word is therefore an *initiating word*; a word that *sets in motion* and *sets in order*.

Kingdom of Priests

Whose prerogative is it to blow the trumpet and sound the advance? '*The sons of Aaron, the priests, shall blow the trumpets*' (Numbers 10:8). Who are the priests of the New Covenant?

> '*You also, as living stones, are being built up a spiritual house, a holy priesthood, to offer up spiritual sacrifices acceptable to God through Jesus Christ.*

> *But you are a chosen generation, a royal priesthood, a holy nation, His own special people, that you may proclaim the praises of Him who called you out of darkness into His marvellous light.'* (1 Peter 2:5, 9)

The new song of redemption, sung before the throne of God and of the Lamb, declares: *'To Him who loved us and washed us from our sins in His own blood, and has made us a kingdom and priests to His God and Father'* (Revelation 1:5, 6).

Every born again, blood-washed, Spirit-filled believer in Jesus is a New Covenant priest after the order of Melchizedek! As priests, we are to offer up spiritual sacrifices to God through Jesus Christ. One of those sacrifices is the ministry of prophetic utterance in the Holy Spirit.

The Apostle Peter, in his 'job description' of the Church, asserts that we are to *'proclaim the praises of Him who called us out of darkness into His marvellous light.'*

The Greek word *'exangello'*, translated 'proclaim', means to *tell out, proclaim abroad, and publish completely*. *'Arete'*, the Greek word translated 'praises', denotes *wonderful deeds, gracious dealings, glorious attributes, virtues, perfections and excellencies*.

The Church is to prophesy out of the vision of Jesus Christ, which is given to her by the Holy Spirit. New Covenant priests are to speak prophetically, by revelation and inspiration of the Holy Spirit, concerning the wonderful acts, glorious attributes and excellent virtues of the Son of God!

As creatures of light, we are to prophesy of the light; speaking glorious things of the divine nature of our heavenly Father. Thus, King David's exhortation to *'sing a new song to the LORD ... bless His Name ... proclaim the good news of His salvation from day to day ... declare His Glory among the nations, His wonders among the people'* (Psalm 96), takes on prophetic significance.

The new song is a song of heart revelation. The spiritual

sacrifices of the royal priesthood include *'psalms, hymns and spiritual songs'* (Ephesians 5:19). Spiritual songs are literally, 'prophetic songs of the Spirit'. According to W.E. Vine, 'spiritual songs are songs of which the burden is the things revealed by the Spirit.'

Spiritual songs, or prophetic songs of the Spirit, are predicated on a sensitivity to the will of God through a constant infilling of the Holy Spirit. *'Understand or perceive what the will of the LORD is, and be being filled with the Holy Spirit'* (Ephesians 5:17, 18).

The Prophetic Word speaks to both the power and the nature of God. It declares the wonderful works of God – that which He has done, is doing, and will yet do. It extols the perfections of His holy character – the attitudes and motivations of His heart toward mankind.

Furthermore, the Prophetic Word casts light on the pathway of the righteous. It gives knowledge of God himself, and of His plans and purposes for the Church, Israel and the nations. Such knowledge prepares and empowers the Body of Messiah to move forward in the Spirit of the Lord.

The ministry of prophetic utterance is the potential province of all New Covenant believers. To the Church at Corinth, the Apostle Paul wrote:

> *'Pursue love, and desire spiritual gifts, but especially that you may prophesy ... I wish you all spoke with tongues, but even more that you prophesied ... For you all can prophesy one by one, that all may learn and all may be encouraged.'*　　　(1 Corinthians 14:1, 5, 31)

Moses envisaged a day of grace when the Church would function as a prophetic community and the Spirit of prophecy would rest upon each believer: *'Oh, that all the LORD's people were prophets and that the LORD would put His Spirit upon them!'* (Numbers 11:29).

The 'Pentecostal Preacher' of the old covenant, Joel, also foresaw the outpouring of the Holy Spirit in the last days:

'And it shall come to pass afterward that I will pour out My Spirit on all flesh; your sons and your daughters shall prophesy, your old men shall dream dreams, your young men shall see visions; And also on My menservants and on My maidservants I will pour out My Spirit in those days.'   (Joel 2:28, 29)

The hallmark of this outpouring is *a universal distribution of the Spirit*: God pouring His Spirit out on *'all flesh'*, not just Jewish flesh! People of all nations coming to the Messiah and partaking of the salvation of the Lord!

'Sons and daughters, menservants and maidservants' prophesying, not just prophets, priests and kings. Prophecy flowing in the kitchen, the workplace and the bedroom, not just in the Synagogue or the Temple.

The presence of the Spirit in the hearts of the redeemed ones as a fountain of revelation knowledge, issuing in a flood of prophetic utterances!

Standing up with the eleven disciples on the day of Pentecost, Peter declared: *'These are not drunk as you suppose ... This is what was spoken by the prophet Joel!'* (Acts 2:15, 16). Unlearned fishermen, ex-prostitutes and tax collectors, former publicans and sinners, 'country bumpkins' from Galilee, each declaring in unknown tongues the wonderful works of God! A new day of prophetic utterance had indeed dawned!

Let God Arise!

The role of the Prophetic Word in initiating a new move forward is demonstrated in the journeyings of Israel through the wilderness.

The presence of God, manifested in a cloud by day and a pillar of fire by night, was the pace-setter in every movement of the camp. As spiritual leader of the people, Moses had to keep his eyes on the cloud at all times!

We know from the record of his prayers how much Moses depended on the presence of God. On one occasion he cried, *'If Your Presence does not go with us, do not bring us up from here'* (Exodus 33:15).

When the cloud was taken up from above the Tabernacle and the Ark of the Covenant set out to find a resting place for the people of Israel, Moses would stand in the midst of the camp and proclaim: *'Rise up, O LORD! Let Your enemies be scattered, and let those who hate You flee before You.'*

Later, when the glory cloud and the holy Ark came to rest in the location of God's choosing, Moses would say: *'Return, O LORD, to the many thousands of Israel'* (Numbers 10:35, 36).

The Prophetic Word addresses the activity of the Spirit of God in the invisible realm; it describes the movement of the glory and presence of the Lord; it teaches people of God's ways, thereby enabling them to walk in His paths.

New Testament prophecy functions in a similar vein, inasmuch as it speaks to the movement of God's Spirit in the life of the congregation. The Apostle Paul said:

> *'For you can all prophesy one by one, that all may learn and all may be encouraged.'*   (1 Corinthians 14:31)

When the Prophetic Word is functioning in divine order and under the anointing of the Holy Spirit, people learn of God – of His nature and power, His ways and dealings, and His plans and purposes. Revelation speaks to a congregation's faith, thereby encouraging them to move on in the vision of the Lord!

Chapter 2

Prophesying the Vision of the Lord

In the year that King Uzziah died, Isaiah saw the Lord. The vision of the Lord, high and lifted up and seated on the throne, changed his life forever. The revelation of God's Glory and the corresponding transformation in Isaiah's character gave birth to a ministry of signs, wonders and prophetic utterance.

> 'Then I said: "Woe is me; for I am undone! Because I am a man of unclean lips, and I dwell in the midst of a people of unclean lips; for my eyes have seen the King, the LORD of Hosts."
>
> Then one of the seraphim flew to me, having in his hand a live coal which he had taken with his tongs from the altar.
>
> And he touched my mouth with it, and said: "Behold, this has touched your lips; your iniquity is taken away, and your sin purged."
>
> Also I heard the voice of the LORD, saying: "Whom shall I send, and who will go for us?" Then I said, "Here am I! Send me."
>
> And He said, "Go, and tell this people..."'
>
> (Isaiah 6:5–9a)

Isaiah prophesied out of the vision of the Lord. His prophetic utterances were inspired by the Spirit through a personal revelation of the holiness and majesty of almighty God.

The first verse of the book of Isaiah summarizes the prophetic ministry of a man which spanned more than forty years and encompassed the reign of four kings of Judah: *'The **vision** of Isaiah the son of Amoz, which he **saw** concerning Judah and Jerusalem in the days of Uzziah, Jotham, Ahaz, and Hezekiah, kings of Judah.'*

And again, in Isaiah 2:1: *'The **word** that Isaiah the son of Amoz **saw** concerning Judah and Jerusalem.'* The key words are *'vision'*, *'word'* and *'saw'*. Vision is the matrix of prophecy!

Prophecy is the speaking forth of that which one sees and hears in the realm of the Spirit; it is the articulation of the vision of Jesus Christ!

The Testimony of Jesus

The book of Revelation is one of the most remarkable pieces of prophetic literature in the Bible. It is, without doubt, a book of prophecy – both the 'forth-telling' of spiritual realities and the 'fore-telling' of future events.

Yet this book of prophecy, by virtue of its very title and introduction, is a ***revelation of Jesus Christ!*** Thank God, it is not a revelation of the antichrist, or of Armageddon, or of the end of the world; it is a revelation of Jesus Christ as the triumphant Lamb of God upon the throne!

> *'The revelation of Jesus Christ, which God gave Him to show His servants – things which must shortly take place. And He sent and signified it by His angel to His servant John,*
>
> *Who bore witness to the Word of God, and to the Testimony of Jesus Christ, and to all things that He saw.*
>
> *Blessed is he who reads and those who hear the words of this prohecy, and keep those things which are written in it; for the time is near.'*   (Revelation 1:1–3)

All prophecy, whether it be forth-telling or fore-telling, should issue from a revelation of Jesus Christ. Like Isaiah, John prophesied out of vision – a vision of the Lamb of God, high and lifted up and seated on the throne!

The prophecy of John was a witness to the Word of God, to the testimony of Jesus, and to all things that he saw in the vision of the Lord. God wanted His servants to have a revelation of the Lamb upon the throne, for that alone would give them the power to endure and overcome. God knew that without such a vision, His people would perish!

Friends, if that was true of the First Century Church, then it is just as true of us today. May God once again give us a revelation of Jesus Christ. Let us see Him crowned with glory and honour, with all things under His feet; King of Kings and Lord of Lords; glorious Head of the Church, full of grace and truth!

Such is the nature and purpose of prophecy. Holy men and women of God, being moved by the Holy Spirit, speaking out of the vision of the risen Lord and causing the people of God to 'see' their Redeemer.

The testimony of Jesus is the spirit and intent of prophecy (Revelation 19:10). Holy Spirit inspired prophecy exalts and magnifies Jesus! The ministry of prophecy is the voice of the Holy Spirit, declaring to the Church the glories and virtues of the Son of God (John 16:14, 15).

If prophecy magnifies the power of the devil and instils fear in the hearts of God's people, it is not true prophecy from the Spirit of God. The gift of prophecy builds up the Church in faith toward God and the Lord Jesus Christ by articulating the vision of the Lord, thereby enlarging people's understanding of His greatness.

The book of Revelation was intended to be read aloud in the churches as a complete manuscript, not dissected by 'prophecy buffs' and pasted on time charts.

If one lifts individual scriptures out of their contextual setting, studying the book to ascertain whether or not the Church is destined to go through the tribulation, or to discover the identity of the antichrist, one misses the whole thrust of the prophecy.

When taken as a whole, without preconceived interpretative notions, the book of Revelation will imbue one with an unshakable faith in the sovereignty of God and the ultimacy of His kingdom! One closes the book, knowing that no matter what happens, God is in control, Jesus is Lord, and His eternal purpose is being outworked in the affairs of men and nations! Hallelujah!

In the Local Church

Christianity has sometimes been called, 'The Great Confession.' The proclamation of truth is an essential part of the life of faith.

We are saved through the belief in and confession of Jesus as Lord (Romans 10:9); Jesus is the Apostle and High Priest of our confession of faith (Hebrews 3:1); and we are to hold fast our confession of hope without wavering, because of God's faithfulness (Hebrews 10:23).

Our mission as Christians is to witness to truth, the truth as it is in Jesus (Acts 1:8). The confession of faith is not a positive statement of personal aspiration; for example, 'I'm believing God for a new Cadillac.' The apostles never made those kind of self-aggrandizing claims, and neither should we.

The 'confession' of which the apostle speaks, is the confession of faith toward God through the Lord Jesus Christ. It is the 'testimony of Jesus' – the testimony of who Jesus is and what He has done. We should be making that kind of confession every day of our lives!

> *'Paul, called to be an apostle of Jesus Christ through the will of God, and Sosthenes our brother,*
>
> *To the Church of God which is at Corinth, to those who are sanctified in Christ Jesus, called to be saints, with all who in every place call on the Name of Jesus Christ our LORD, both theirs and ours.'*

(1 Corinthians 1:1, 2)

True Christians are those who are set apart unto God through the Blood of Jesus and the power of the Holy Spirit, and who *'call on the Name of Jesus Christ the Lord.'*

The same Greek formula that Paul uses in 1 Corinthians 1:2 is also used in Genesis 12:8 and 13:4 in the Septuagint (the Greek translation of the Old Testament) to denote **worship** and **prayer**: *'There he (Abram) built an altar to the LORD and called on the Name of the Lord.'*

No one can say, with understanding and conviction, *'Jesus is Lord,'* except by inspiration of the Holy Spirit (1 Corinthians 12:3). In other words, the Holy Spirit comes into the life of a believer for the express purpose of administering the Lordship of Jesus. The evidence of His presence is the believer's proclamation of the Lord Jesus.

Joel declared that the outpouring of the Spirit upon all flesh would issue in a torrent of mighty prophetic utterances (Joel 2:28). When the disciples were filled with the Holy Spirit on the day of Pentecost, they spoke in a variety of personally unknown tongues, declaring the wonderful works of God (Acts 2:11).

When the household of Cornelius received the gift of salvation and the Holy Spirit, they spoke with tongues and magnified God (Acts 10:46). And when Paul laid his hands on the disciples at Ephesus, the Holy Spirit came upon them and they spoke with tongues and prophesied (Acts 19:6).

Speaking (or singing) in unknown tongues and prophetic utterance is the point of overflow in the Life of the Spirit: *'... be filled with the Spirit, speaking to one another in psalms, hymns and spiritual songs, singing and making melody in your heart to the Lord, giving thanks always for all things to God the Father in the Name of our Lord Jesus Christ'* (Ephesians 5:18–20).

The 'grace of prophetic utterance' should be flowing in every local assembly of God's people.

> *'I thank my God always concerning you for the grace of God which was given to you by Christ Jesus, that you*

were enriched in everything by Him in all utterance and all knowledge.

Even as the testimony of Christ was confirmed in you, so that you come short in no gift, eagerly waiting for the revelation of our Lord Jesus Christ.'

(1 Corinthians 1:4–7)

The Greek word '*ploutizo*', translated 'enrich', means to *make wealthy*, and speaks of *fullness or abundance*. The will of God for every local church is that they may be enriched and made wealthy, not just in finance and material possessions, but in 'all kinds of utterance' and 'all realms of knowledge,' for the sake of the testimony of Christ.

All kinds of utterance and all realms of knowledge must undoubtedly include '*prophetic utterance*' and '*revelation knowledge*', especially as this statement appears in an epistle that deals explicitly with the operation of the supernatural gifts of the Holy Spirit in the Church.

God does not will for His people to come short in *any* gift. He has blessed us with every spiritual blessing in the heavenly realms in Christ (Ephesians 1:3). The manifestation of the Spirit is given to each member for the general profit of the whole Body (1 Corinthians 12:7).

Because of sin, mankind has *fallen short* (Gk: '*hustereo*') of the glory of God (Romans 3:23). But through His great grace, the Father of glory has redeemed us, recreated us, and called us to His eternal glory by Christ Jesus (1 Peter 5:10).

God has made abundant provision; therefore, we should not *come short* (Gk: '*hustereo*') in any spiritual gift, as we eagerly await the revelation of the Lord Jesus from heaven!

Through the gifts of the Spirit, we are restored to the realm of the glory of God! Prophetic utterance and revelation knowledge lifts one up into the dimension of the Spirit where one thinks God's thoughts, speaks God's words, and performs God's works.

The goal of the operation of the Spirit, and of the prophetic ministry in particular, is to confirm the testimony of

Christ in His people. As we have noted, the testimony of Jesus – the declaration of His glorious virtues and excellent greatness – is the *spirit* of prophecy.

The Greek word *'bebaioo'*, translated 'confirm', means to *stabilitate, make firm, establish, and make secure*. It is derived from the Greek word *'basis'* (from which we get the English words 'base' and 'basis'), which means *a pace*, and by implication speaks of *the foot*. Therefore, the word structure of 'confirm' contains the idea of *basality*.

Prophetic utterances of the Spirit in the local church help to establish the vision of the glorified and ascended Christ in the hearts and minds of God's people.

Whether we realize it or not, the vision we have of Jesus constitutes the foundation of our Christian life. Without a clear and *progressive* vision of the Lord Jesus as He is *today*, at the Father's right hand, God's people dwell carelessly, wander aimlessly, and are tossed about like waves of the sea.

> *'As you have therefore received Christ Jesus the Lord, so walk in Him, rooted and built up in Him and established in the faith, as you have been taught, abounding in it with thanksgiving.'*   (Colossians 2:6, 7)

Prophesying out of the vision of the Lord disseminates revelation, quickens understanding, and releases faith among the congregation.

Prophecy is a necessary complement to the systematic teaching of the Scriptures, and when thus combined, accedes to a unity of the faith in the knowledge of the Son of God, the end of which is a mature man, measured according to the full standard of Christ's perfection (Ephesians 4:13).

A Spirit of Seeing

The prophets of the Old Covenant were also called 'seers' (1 Samuel 9:9), because of their ability to see into the invisible realm and discern spiritual realities. One such man was the hireling-prophet Balaam, who possessed awesome prophetic insight and foresight, albeit with grave flaws in his personal morality and integrity.

> *'The utterance of Balaam the son of Beor, and the utterance of the man whose eyes are opened; the utterance of him who hears the Word of God, and knows the knowledge of the Most High, who sees the vision of the Almighty, who falls down with eyes opened wide:*
>
> *I see Him, but not now; I behold Him, but not near; a Star shall come out of Jacob; a Sceptre shall rise out of Israel...'* (Numbers 24:15–17)

Balaam's eyes were opened wide to see the vision of the almighty. That 'vision of the Almighty' included the birth of Messiah Jesus, the 'Star of Jacob' and the 'Sceptre of Israel', approximately 1,450 years later! Because of this long-range perception, the Jerusalem Bible calls Balaam, *'the man with far-seeing eyes.'*

The Hebrew word *'galah'*, translated 'open wide', means to *denude, uncover and unveil*. The Holy Spirit is the Spirit of revelation or unveiling, who enlightens the eyes of our understanding in the knowledge of the Lord (Ephesians 1:17–19).

He removes the veil that we might see the vision of the Lord, and in seeing His vision, gaze worshipfully upon His glory, and in gazing upon His glory, be transformed into His image!

> *'Nevertheless when one turns to the Lord, the veil is taken away. Now the Lord is the Spirit; and where the Spirit of the Lord is, there is liberty.*
>
> *But we all, with unveiled face, beholding as in a mirror the glory of the Lord, are being transformed into the same image from glory to glory, just as by the Spirit of the Lord.'* (2 Corinthians 3:16–18)

There is a 'Spirit of seeing' that descends upon God's people from time to time. I have been in meetings where the 'Spirit of seeing' or the 'Spirit of prophetic vision' has fallen upon whole congregations. Throughout the room, men and women spontaneously and simultaneously saw the vision of the glory of God!

Such supernatural happenings are often catalysed by prophetic utterances, delivered in the midst of real spiritual worship. The Prophetic Word 'opens a door in heaven', as it were, and catches people up in the Spirit to the throne of grace, where they see the vision and hear the word of the Lord.

Elisha's servant arose one morning and went out of his master's house in Dothan, only to discover that the city was surrounded by the horses and chariots of the Syrian army.

In great alarm, the servant returned to the house and said, *'Alas, my master! What shall we do?'* Elisha answered, *'Do not fear, for those who are with us are more than those who are with them.'*

Then Elisha prayed, *'Lord, open his eyes that he may see.'* Like the drawing of a curtain, the Lord opened the young man's eyes, and he saw into the realm of the Spirit. And behold, the mountain was full of horses and chariots of fire – the hosts of heaven – all around Elisha! (2 Kings 6:15–17).

Such is the nature and such is the purpose of the Prophetic Word: to open the eyes of the blind that they may see the reality of God in the realm of the Spirit.

May it be our prayer today. 'Lord, open our eyes that we may see!'

Chapter 3

Prophesying Divine Encouragement

In the kingdom of God, as in all of life, there is a premium on courage. The moral faculty of courage is often the difference between great success and miserable failure, heroic victory and cowardly defeat.

'Courage' is that quality of spirit which enables one to obey God and perform exploits in His Name. To the newly appointed commander of Israel, Joshua, the Lord said: *'Only be strong and very courageous that you may observe to do...'*

'Courage' is an act; daring to act on God's Word; daring to do that which God tells one to do. The New Testament concept of boldness is akin to the Old Testament concept of courage. One of the Greek words translated as 'boldness', *'tolmao'*, signifies to *dare to do*.

Every soldier experiences feelings of doubt, fear and uncertainty. Everyone's knees knock together at one time or another. However, the difference between the men and the boys is the act of putting one's life on the line in the heat of battle.

Both the hero and the coward feel a knot in the stomach, goosebumps on the arm and a chill in the spine. But the hero disregards his feelings and the possible consequences of his action, and plunges into the fray. He simply grits his teeth and does it!

Meanwhile, the coward stands on the sidelines and counts the cost, and counts, and counts, and counts ... and never acts!

God eliminated such people from Gideon's army: those who were bound by fear and those who were paralysed by self-preservation. Gideon was left with a band of three hundred desperate men, who committed to watch and act when he gave the signal (Judges 6 & 7).

The Bible always associates courage and boldness with *action!* Paul and Barnabas epitomized holy courage, in that they *'risked their lives for the name of the Lord Jesus Christ'* (Acts 15:26). They preached boldly, travelled boldly, lived boldly, and died boldly, for the glory of God!

The aged prophet-king, David, said to his young son and successor, Solomon: *'Be strong and of good courage, **and do it**; do not fear nor be dismayed, for the LORD God – my God – will be with you. He will not leave you nor forsake you, until you have finished all the work for the service of the House of the LORD'* (1 Chronicles 28:20).

'Courage' is an element of the divine nature, implanted in the heart of man by the Holy Spirit. The infilling of the Holy Spirit always issues in words and actions of courageous faith. *'... they were all filled with the Holy Spirit and they spoke the Word of God with boldness'* (Acts 4:31).

Spiritual Alertness

The Hebrew word *'amats'*, translated 'courage', is a primary root meaning *to be alert*. It denotes a state of *spiritual and moral alertness, strength, firmness, solidity and boldness*.

The Lord said to Joshua,

> *'Have I not commanded you? Be strong and of good courage; do not be afraid, nor be dismayed, for the LORD your God is with you wherever you go.'*
>
> (Joshua 1:9)

It is interesting to note alternative translations of this Divine injunction. Dr James Moffatt reads: *'These are My orders: Be firm and brave...'* The New English Bible says:

'*... be strong and resolute...*' But perhaps the most striking of all versions is that of Monsignor Ronald Knox:

> '*Courage and a man's part, that is what I ask of thee; no room for fear and shrinking back, when the Lord thy God is at thy side wherever thou goest.*'

The antithetical forces of courage and cowardice are clearly illustrated in the animal world, in the contrasting behaviour of the eagle and the ostrich.

When trouble comes, the coward, like the ostrich, buries his head in the sand, pretending that it doesn't exist or hoping that it will go away. He closes his eyes so that he cannot see the truth, seeking refuge in the illusionary world of ignorance. And when cornered, he would rather flee than fight, being obsessed with the instinct of self-preservation.

On the other hand, the man of courage, like the eagle, has amazing powers of perception. He is constantly alert, scrutinizing the horizon and analyzing what he sees. When danger threatens, he is well prepared. He may not launch an immediate frontal assault, but instead, will back up and wait for an opportunity to strike a fatal blow against the intruder.

Christians are called to be eagles, not ostriches. '*Those who wait on the LORD shall renew their strength; they shall rise up with wings like eagles...*' (Isaiah 40:31). Waiting and worshipping in the presence of the Lord sharpens one's spiritual perception, thus enabling one to see the issues as God sees them.

When one's eyes are opened to see the issues as God sees them, one can then receive His plan of action. '*The people who know their God will display strength and take action*' (Daniel 11:32, NASB). Courageous action is the result of spiritual perception!

The watchman who sees evidence of an imminent attack, takes steps to courageously defend his city. The essence of courage is *alertness!*

In his letter to the Church of Corinth, the Apostle Paul describes various elements which, taken together, constitute spiritual courage:

> *'Watch, stand fast in the faith, be brave, be strong.'*
> (1 Corinthians 16:13)

The Greek word *'gregoreuo'*, translated 'watch', means to *keep awake and be vigilant*. It is derived from another word *'egeiro'*, which means to *rouse from sleep and to collect one's faculties*. The word picture is of a sentry, wide awake and in full control of his faculties, maintaining a constant vigil at the gate and on the wall.

Moreover, such a one stands firm in the faith, withstanding every onslaught of evil, refusing to compromise an inch of ground, either through intimidation or deception. The Watchman is called to *act manly* or *play the man* (Gk: *'andrizomai'*) in the face of evil; to display the manly vigour of Messiah in all His Glory!

Finally, the Watchman is to 'be strong'. According to the Expositor's Greek Testament, this 'enjoins manful activity in its most energetic form,' and signifies 'superior power, mastery,' not merely strong, but 'mighty.' Furthermore, it denotes a process of development, to 'grow in strength' and 'increase in vigour.'

Hearing from Heaven

It takes courage to enter into the Land of Promise and possess one's inheritance in God. The Lord said to Joshua, *'Be strong and of good courage, for to this people you shall give as a possession the land which I swore to their fathers to give them'* (Joshua 1:6).

More often than not, there are giants to contend with before we can *'live in houses that we have not built, drink of wells that we have not dug, and eat the fruit of vineyards that we have not planted.'*

The land might be flowing with milk and honey, but the

milk and honey is not on tap. The children of Israel had to milk the cows and rob the bees, and unfortunately, the cows and the bees belonged to people who did not share the vision of the Abrahamic Covenant, nor did they believe in giving and receiving!

As the Apostle Paul discovered, whenever God opens a great and effective door to the gospel, there is bound to be many adversaries (1 Corinthians 16:9). This bespeaks warfare, of which an essential requisite is courage!

The Word of God is the generator of courageous faith. When God speaks, faith and courage automatically appear. The Bible contains many life stories of heroes of faith – ordinary men and women with ordinary weaknesses and limitations, who performed daring and mighty feats to the glory of God.

Yet, all of these saints were human beings with a nature such as you and I have. What transformed them into men and women of faith and power? **The Word of God!** Again and again we read this phrase: *'And the Lord said to Abraham ... And the Lord said to Moses ... And the Lord said to Gideon ... And the Lord said to David...'*

God's words are Spirit and life; each word contains within itself the 'Breath' of the Almighty, the creative nature and power of the living God (John 6:63). Through the exceedingly great and precious promises of God, we partake of the divine nature (2 Peter 1:4).

When God speaks, life is imparted. Courage. Faith. Hope. Vision. Strength. Power. And men's hearts are changed. Ordinary people become extraordinary. Natural people perform supernatural exploits.

A case in point is Polycarp, a godly saint and church father of the Second Century. As a disciple of St. John, Polycarp was the last surviving link with the original apostles. He served for many years, in a most distinguished fashion, as Bishop of the Church at Smyrna.

At the height of a devastating persecution in the Roman Province of Asia, the aged Polycarp was arrested. Three days before he was seized, in a vision at night and during prayer, the pillow under his head seemed to suddenly catch fire and be consumed.

Waking out of his sleep, Polycarp immediately began to interpret the vision to those present, almost foretelling the event that was about to take place, and plainly declaring to those around him that it would be necessary for him to give up his life in the flames for Christ's sake.

Therefore, when the soldiers came for him, he did not resist or seek to escape, but ordered a table to be prepared for the men, encouraged them to eat well, and begged of them that he might pray undisturbed. Having received permission, he arose and prayed, so full of the grace of the Lord that those present who heard him were amazed, and many of them repented that so venerable and pious a man should be put to death.

Polycarp was then conducted to the stadium, where many thousands of people had gathered to indulge in an orgy of lust and murder. As he entered the arena, the crowd, drunk with the blood of martyrs and saints, erupted into a cacophonous frenzy.

In the midst of the uproar, a voice spoke from heaven: *'Be strong, Polycarp, and contend manfully.'* No one saw who it was that spoke; but the voice itself was heard by many of the believers.

Polycarp was then led forth to the Proconsul, who sought to persuade him to renounce Christ. 'Eighty six years have I served Him,' Polycarp replied, 'And He never did me wrong; How can I now blaspheme my King that has saved me?'

Thus maintaining his apology of faith, Polycarp was bound to the stake and the fire was lit. However, the flames appeared unable to consume the Man of God, forming a wall around his body like the sail of a vessel filled with wind.

Finally, the executioner drew near and plunged his sword into the martyr, and when he had done this, such a quantity of blood gushed forth that the fire was extinguished, to the astonishment of all the spectators.

In like manner, the Lord Jesus spoke to the Apostle Paul in a night vision during a time of great stress and uncertainty:

> *'Do not be afraid, but speak, and do not keep silent; for I am with you, and no one will attack you to hurt you; for I have many people in this city.'*   (Acts 18:9, 10)

The 'voice from heaven' gave Paul the necessary strength and courage to continue teaching the Word of God in Corinth for a further eighteen months!

When Paul was arrested in Jerusalem and his life was threatened by the unbelieving Jews, the Lord stood by him and said:

> *'Be of good cheer, Paul; for as you have testified of Me in Jerusalem, so you must also bear Witness at Rome.'*
> (Acts 23:11)

It is important to understand that the Lord was not merely telling Paul to be of good cheer; Jesus' words actually imparted cheer and courage! In reality, the Lord was saying: **'Paul, here is My courage, receive it. Here is My faith, receive it. Here is My power, receive it!'** Of His fullness have we all received, and grace upon grace! (John 1:16)

Speaking Edification

Hearing from God, whether through Scripture, the witness of the Spirit, vision, dream or prophetic utterance, releases faith and produces courage.

The primary purpose of the New Testament gift of prophecy is to *edify* the Church. For this reason, we are admonished to desire all spiritual gifts, but *especially* the gift of prophecy, because this gift is of the greatest benefit to the whole Body.

> *'But he who prophesies speaks edification and exhortation and comfort to men. He who speaks in a tongue*

edifies himself, but he who prophesies edifies the Church.

I wish you all spoke with tongues, but even more that you prophesied; for he who prophesies is greater than he who speaks with tongues, unless indeed he interprets, that the Church may receive edification.

For you can all prophesy one by one, that all may learn and all may be encouraged.'

(1 Corinthians 14:3–5, 31)

The Greek word *'oikodome'*, translated 'edification', is an architectural term that denotes the act of building. In Old Enligh the word 'edify' was used in its original sense of *build*. Thus Wycliffe renders Genesis 2:22, *'The Lord God edified the rib which He took of Adam, into a woman.'* The Latin *'aedificare'*, from which our English word is derived, means to *build a house*.

The Prophetic Word is an indispensable tool for the building up of the Church in faith toward God and love for one another. Prophecy is the speaking forth of the mind of God in a specific situation, which speech gives life, imparts grace, and generates faith.

The Apostle Paul admonished Timothy not to neglect the spiritual gift that was in him, which was given to him *by prophecy* with the laying on of the hands of the presbytery (1 Timothy 4:14). Prophecy is the transference of God's riches in glory into the lives of His people, through the medium of the spoken word.

Prophecy is the speaking forth, by the inspiration of the Holy Spirit, of that which is good for necessary edification (Ephesians 4:29). Through the prophetic anointing, individual members and entire communities are built up on the foundation of the most holy faith (Jude 20). Spiritual atmospheres are changed, revelatory understanding dawns, and victory is assured.

From time to time I have been in prayer meetings where people prayed from the perspective of need. In prayer, they told God all about the need (as if He didn't already know).

30

The more they talked about the need, the more impossible it appeared, until every ounce of faith and courage was consumed.

Thank God, in some of these situations the Holy Spirit mercifully intervened with a flash of prophetic revelation that turned the prayer meeting upside down (or right side up!) As God's mind was declared, faith was released. People began to see through God's eyes and think with God's thoughts. Invariably, a spirit of joyous victory pervaded the meeting!

The declaration of God's mind releases God's energy and authority among His people. It lifts them up into heavenly places, where Jesus is Lord and all things are possible. It opens the fountains of God's grace and love, and causes His river to flow in the midst of the Church.

In the words of the New English Bible, *'It is prophecy that builds up a Christian community!'*

Exhortation...

The Greek word *'paraklesis'*, translated 'exhortation', literally means *a calling to one's side to help*. It is used in the sense of imploration, entreaty, admonition and solace, thus denoting *consolatory exhortation*.

The Holy Spirit is the great exhorter (Gk: *'paraklete'*). His ministry of comfort goes far deeper than the mere soothing of hurts and heartaches. 'Comfort' is derived from the Latin *'comfortare'*, *to make strong*. Thus, the exhortation of the Spirit is designed to strengthen us for service and galvanize us into prophetic action.

The Spirit implores, entreats, admonishes, comforts and consoles, *through the Prophetic Word!* When God speaks, we are strengthened to do the work of the Kingdom (Daniel 10:19). This is the essence of divine encouragement.

Thank God, there is a word of exhortation in the Holy Spirit, that gives strength to the weary and courage to the faint-hearted (Isaiah 50:4). The Prophetic Word is indeed, *'like apples of gold in pictures of silver'* (Proverbs 25:11).

> *'Now Judas and Silas, themselves being prophets also, exhorted the brethren with many words and strengthened them.'* (Acts 15:32)

On many occasions I have personally experienced the redeeming and rejuvenating power of a Prophetic Word, spoken under the anointing of the Holy Spirit. In some instances it has meant the difference between quitting and continuing in the ministry.

The Bible contains many examples of individuals being inspired and strengthened to continue in the work of the Lord through a word of prophecy. The reform-minded King of Judah, Asa, was encouraged in the quest for national revival by the prophet Oded: *'But you, be strong and do not let your hands be weak, for your work shall be rewarded!'*

When Asa heard these words and the prophecy of Oded, he took courage and removed the abominable idols from all the land, and restored the altar of the Lord! (2 Chronicles 15:8).

Some three hundred years later, the King of Babylon laid siege to Jerusalem, destroyed the Temple, and carried the surviving inhabitants into exile. But in fulfilment of the word spoken by Jeremiah the prophet, a remnant of the people returned to the land after an absence of seventy years, to rebuild the waste places and raise up the foundations of many generations.

Upon their return, one of the first projects undertaken by the people was the rebuilding of the Temple. The foundation was laid in 536 BC amidst great joy and weeping, but due to local hostility and other hardships, the people soon halted construction and became preoccupied with their own building programmes.

Sixteen years later, God sent His prophets, Haggai and Zechariah, to exhort the people to get back to the task of

building His House. It is interesting to read the prophecies
of Haggai and Zechariah in this light.

> *'Then Haggai, the LORD's messenger, spoke the LORD's*
> *message to the people, saying, 'I am with you, says the*
> *LORD.'*
> *So the LORD stirred up the spirit of Zerubbabel the*
> *son of Shealtiel, Governor of Judah, and the spirit of*
> *Joshua the son of Jehozadak, the High Priest, and the*
> *spirit of all the remnant of the people; and they came*
> *and worked on the house of the LORD of Hosts, their*
> *God.'* (Haggai 1:13, 14)

The Word of the Lord, spoken by Haggai, stirred up the
spirit of the leaders and the people to take prophetic action.
It was a 'red hot word' that brought conviction, produced
repentance and provoked obedience.

One of the major hindrances to the work of the kingdom
is procrastination. Satan tries to persuade us to 'put off
until tomorrow' what God would have us do today! In the
case of the returning exiles, it was the notion that *'the time
has not come to build the LORD's house'* (Haggai 1:2).

The Hebrew word *'uwr'*, translated 'stir up', means to
wake up, and hence, to *rouse oneself to activity*. The Prophetic Word is an *awakening word*, a *delivering word*, and a
precipitating word. It awakens from spiritual slumber,
delivers from the bondage of procrastination and precipitates obedient action!

> *'Then the prophet Haggai and Zechariah the son of*
> *Iddo, prophets, prophesied to the Jews who were in*
> *Judah and Jerusalem, in the Name of the God of Israel,*
> *who was over them.*
> *So Zerubbabel the son of Shealtiel and Joshua the*
> *son of Jozadak rose up and began to build the house of*
> *God which is in Jerusalem; and the prophets of God*
> *were with them, helping them.'* (Ezra 5:1, 2)

Once again, we see prophecy functioning as a *supportive word* that undergirds the people of God as they do the Work of the Kingdom; a *stimulating word* that causes God's people to put their hands to the plow and not look back; a *refreshing word* that revives the weary soul and replenishes one's strength for the journey.

All of these meanings are contained in the Hebrew word '*caad*', which describes the action of the Prophetic Word in 'helping' the Jews to build the Temple.

And Comfort ...

'*Paramuthia*', the Greek word translated 'comfort', is *a word that comes to the side of one to stimulate or comfort him*, hence, *an exhortation or encouragement*. It denotes *a persuasive address* and *an incentive appeal*. The word also contains the idea of *tenderness* and *assuagement*, hence, *consolation*.

The Prophetic Word is a *healing word* that conveys the restorative love of God to broken hearts and battered lives; a *hopeful word* that lifts up the head of the one who is bowed down, thus causing him or her to see something of the glorious future that God has in store for those who love Him.

'*For I know the thoughts that I think toward you, says the LORD, thoughts of peace and not of evil, to give you a future and a hope*' (Jeremiah 29:11). Through the Prophetic Word, God speaks to His people of that future hope, and enlightens the eyes of their hearts to behold the destiny that awaits them in Messiah Jesus!

> '*If, then, any encouragement comes through union with Christ, if there is any persuasive power in love, if there is any communion with the Spirit ...*'
>
> (Philippians 2:1, TCNT)

Paul's statement is purely rhetorical. There is divine encouragement through union with Christ; there is a tender power of persuasion in God's love; there is communion with the Holy Spirit! Hallelujah! Many times God ministers His love and encouragement to us, and communes with us, in His Prophetic Word.

For this reason, Paul says: *'You can all prophesy one by one, that all may learn and all may be encouraged'* (1 Corinthians 14:31).

It is Jesus, our gracious Saviour and gentle Shepherd, who is speaking to His Church through the gift of the Holy Spirit. *'A bruised reed He will not break, and smoking flax He will not quench'* (Isaiah 42:3). Rather, *'He will gather the lambs with His arm, and carry them in His bosom, and gently lead those who are with young'* (Isaiah 40:11).

The Spirit of prophecy is the Spirit of the Good Shepherd, feeding, gathering, carrying, and gently leading His people.

Prophesy, and be an instrument of the Lord's encouragement for the building up of His Church!

Chapter 4

Prophesying Resurrection Life

'Man shall not live by bread alone,' said Jesus, *'but by every word that proceeds from the mouth of God'* (Matthew 4:4).

The Lord God is the source, the possessor, and the giver of life. That life is contained in and communicated through His *Words*.

> *'It is the Spirit who gives Life; the flesh profits nothing. The words that I speak to you are Spirit, and they are Life.'* (John 6:63)

No Word of God is void of power (Luke 1:37). Every utterance of God contains within itself the seed of His divine nature and the potential of His creative power. The Word of God has the ability to bring itself to pass!

As one meditates on the promises of God, thus allowing his spirit-man to digest them, one actually partakes of the nature of God that is contained in His word (2 Peter 1:4). God's word is living and powerful, exercising supernatural power in the lives of those who believe and obey it!

In the language of the Amplified Bible, *'The Word of God is effectually at work in you who believe, exercising its superhuman power in those who adhere to and trust in and rely on it'* (1 Thessalonians 2:13).

Indeed, the Word of God is the key to spiritual growth. It is able to build the believer up and give him an inheritance among those who are sanctified (Acts 20:32). One's attitude toward the Word is a reflection of one's attitude toward God. The place that the Word holds in one's life is the place that God holds in one's life!

God comes to us through His Word, speaks to us through His Word, communes with us through His Word, reveals Himself through His Word and imparts life through His Word!

It is important for us to recognize that the Word of God both *contains* and *imparts* life. Jesus said, *'I am the Resurrection and the Life,'* and later, *'...if you would believe* (My words) *you would see the Glory of God'* (John 11:25, 40).

The words of Jesus, when believed and acted upon, brought life into the valley of the shadow of death. With a loud voice He cried, *'Lazarus, come forth!'* The life that was in the word penetrated the tomb, entered the decaying body of the deceased, and reversed the process of death!

The principle of 'life through the word' is clearly illustrated in the story of Abraham, who, by virtue of his obedience, became the father of the faithful:

> *...those who are of the faith of Abraham, who is the father of us all*
>
> *(as it is written, 'I have made you a father of many nations') in the presence of Him whom he believed, even God, who gives life to the dead and calls those things which do not exist as though they did;*
>
> *Who, contrary to hope, in hope believed, so that he became the father of many nations, according to what was spoken, 'so shall your descendants be.*

(Romans 4:16–18)

Almighty God gives life to the dead. How? *By calling those things which do not exist as though they did.* By speaking a *word of life* or a *word that contains and imparts life* to those who dwell in the land of the shadow of death.

Death is a spiritual realm and power that affects every aspect of man's existence. Divorce is the working of death in a marriage; a 'generation-gap' between parents and children is the working of death in a family; poverty is the working of death materially; sickness is the working of death physically; depression is the working of death mentally and emotionally.

The realm of death must be invaded and conquered by a superior force: *life!* Jesus came to introduce the life of God to the family of man: *'I have come that they may have Life, and that they may have it more abundantly'* (John 10:10).

Through His death, burial and resurrection, Jesus destroyed (rendered powerless) him who had the power of death, that is the devil, and released those who through fear of death were all their lifetime subject to bondage (Hebrews 2:14, 15).

He is the Prince of Life (Acts 3:15). He is the life-giver. There is life in His Name. There is life in His touch. There is life in His words!

When God speaks, life is imparted! Resurrection life, that conquers death in all its forms. Man is made alive by the Word of God, and man walks in an ever-increasing measure of divine life as he hears and obeys the words that proceed from the mouth of God.

Prophecy in Death Valley

Whether we like it or not, the journey of faith that we are called upon to undertake passes through 'death valley.' Psalm 23, though often read and sung at funerals, is a Psalm for living, not dying! It describes the various experiences of life that we pass through in our walk with the Lord.

'The Lord is my Shepherd, I shall not lack.' No matter what kind of circumstance we encounter, the Lord is our sufficiency. The Lord leads us through good times: *'He makes me lie down in green pastures, He leads me beside still waters,'* and not so good times: *'Yea, though I walk through the valley of the shadow of death.'* But through it all, *'Your rod and Your staff comforts me.'*

The *'valley of the shadow of death'* has nothing whatever

to do with the death of a Christian and his passage into the presence of God. By studying the context of this statement, one discovers that the Shepherd is leading His sheep through territory that is inhabited by hostile enemies.

Lurking in the shadows are ravenous wolves that delight to prey upon defenceless sheep. Consequently, this is a dangerous, but necessary stretch of road to negotiate. For at the end of this sector stands a festive table, adorned with every kind of good and perfect provision. It is the Lord's Feast, prepared for those who overcome adversity.

Those who pass through the tests and trials of 'death valley' will surely come forth into God's prepared place of abundance and glory!

What are we to do when we find ourselves passing through 'death valley'? Should we passively accept the reign of death or are we to invade it with a mandate of life?

Jesus said of the one who believes in Him, that out of his innermost being would flow rivers of living water – the Spirit of the life of God! (John 7:38). The life of God is aggressive and dominant. No matter what situation it finds itself in, *it flows out* – attacking, conquering, and casting out the spirit of death.

The life of God in you, the believer, wants to rise up and attack the spirit of death around you – in all its various forms and manifestations. He who is in you is greater than he who is in the world! (1 John 4:4).

How can we release the life of God in 'death valley'? *Through the Prophetic Word!* Death and life are in the power of the tongue (Proverbs 18:21). When one speaks the *rhema* (quickened Word) of God, life is imparted!

The thirty-seventh chapter of Ezekiel is a classic portrait of the life of God flowing through the Prophetic Word into a valley of death, bringing forth revival and restoration in a humanly impossible situation.

> *'The hand of the LORD came upon me and brought me out in the Spirit of the LORD, and set me down in the midst of the valley; and it was full of bones.*

> *Then He caused me to pass by them all around, and behold, there were very many in the open valley; and inded they were very dry.'*

What a hopeless situation! A valley full of corpses, a mass graveyard, a veritable killing field. These were not recent victims, but anatomical memorials to a distant catastrophe. The flesh was dissolved, the skeletons were disintegrated, and bones were scattered from one end of the valley to the other!

As Ezekiel surveyed this scene of desolation, the Lord said to him, *'Son of Man, can these bones live?'* Conscious of his own inadequacy in the face of such calamity, Ezekiel replied, *'O LORD God, You know.'*

Then the Lord instructed Ezekiel to do a most unusual thing: *'Prophesy to these bones, and say to them, "O dry bones, hear the word of the LORD!"'*

Talk to the bones! Speak to the problem! What an amazing command! Yet, it is remarkably similar to the teaching of the Lord Jesus in Mark 11:23; *'For assuredly, I say to you, Whoever says to this mountain, "Be removed and be cast into the sea," and does not doubt in his heart, but believes that those things he says will come to pass, he will have whatever he says.'*

God's goal is to put His word in the mouths of His people. And it is by the word of the Lord in our mouths that we rule over circumstances of life, making them conform to God's will and pleasure (Jeremiah 1:9, 10).

The power is in the word! The life is in the word! As the Word of God is spoken in faith, the life of God is imparted to the object of His care:

> *'Thus says the LORD God to these bones: "Surely I will cause breath to enter into you, and you shall live.*
>
> *I will put sinews on you and bring flesh upon you, cover you with skin and put breath in you; and you shall live. Then you shall know that I am the LORD."'*

(Ezekiel 37:5, 6)

The Hebrew word *'ruwach'*, translated 'breath', is also translated in other places as *wind*, and *spirit*. It is derived from a primary root which means to *blow* or breathe. Hence, *'ruwach'* denotes *the spirit of life*.

> *'So I prophesied as I was commanded; and as I prophesied, there was a noise, and suddenly a rattling; and the bones came together, bone to bone.*
>
> *Indeed, as I looked, the sinews and the flesh came upon them, and the skin covered them over; but there was no breath in them.*
>
> *Then He said to me, "Prophesy to the breath, prophesy, Son of Man, and say to the breath, 'Thus says the LORD God: "Come from the four winds, O breath, and breathe on these slain, that they may live." ' "*
>
> *So I prophesied as He commanded me, and breath came into them, and they lived, and stood upon their feet, an exceedingly great army.'*   (Ezekiel 37:7–10)

Pay close attention to verse seven, because it contains one of the most important principles of prophetic ministry in the Word of God: *'So I prophesied **as I was commanded;** and **as I prophesied,** there was a noise, and suddenly a rattling; and the bones came together, bone to bone.'*

A prophet is literally, 'one who speaks for another'. The miracle of the gift of prophecy is that redeemed ones like you and I become a voice in the earth for the word of the living God!

The word is God's, the voice is man's. The Word of God is the master, the voice of man is the servant. The prophetic ministry is a valet to the Spirit and the word. We prophesy *as we are commanded*, speaking God's specific word in His specific time.

Jesus constantly ministered in the dynamic of prophetic utterance. Listen to His testimony, and take careful notice of the relationship between the *prophet* and the *word*:

'For I have not spoken on My own authority; but the Father who sent Me gave Me a command, what I should say and what I should speak.

And I know that His command is everlasting life. Therefore, whatever I speak, just as the Father has told Me, so I speak.'   (John 12:49, 50)

Prophecy is not a production of the will of man, but of the Spirit of God. Holy men, whose lives are separated from sin and consecrated unto God, speak on His behalf, being moved and impelled by the Spirit (2 Peter 1:21).

The faithful prophet cannot go beyond the word of the Lord, to do either good or bad of his own will; he must speak and act within the parameters of the revelation of God (Numbers 24:13).

One of the pitfalls of prophetic ministry is the temptation to speculate on the word of the Lord. Once the prophecy has been delivered and the anointing has dissipated, one should not attempt to interpret the word through the process of one's natural reasoning. The Spirit of God and the passage of time are the only bona fide interpreters of the Prophetic Word.

Jesus said, *'The Father who sent Me gave Me a command, what I should say and what I should speak.'* Child of God, if the Lord sends you on a mission, He will tell you what to say: *'He whom God has sent speaks the words of God...'* (John 3:34).

The word that the Lord gives you to speak will generate life in the place to which you are sent. Jesus continued, *'And I know that His command is everlasting life. Therefore, I speak, just as the Father has told Me...'*

When prophesying, one should speak and act out *exactly* what one receives in the Spirit. Don't make the word conform to the demeanour of the congregation; make the congregation conform to the demeanour of the word!

And as you prophesy, life will flow and life will be! Speak the word first, and the signs, wonders and manifestations of the Spirit will follow after, to confirm the counsel of the Lord.

43

Rendezvous in Caesarea

The Lord's way of imparting the life of the Spirit through the Prophetic Word is dramatically demonstrated in the tenth chapter of the Book of Acts.

In obedience to the summons of the Spirit, the Apostle Peter left his place of rest and prayer in Jaffa and travelled up the coast to the Roman military port of Caesarea, to address an extended family gathering in the home of Cornelius.

After welcoming Peter to his home and explaining the supernatural nature of the invitation, Cornelius said: *'Now therefore, we are all present before God to hear all the things commanded you by God.'*

With that, Peter opened his mouth and began to preach the good news of Jesus the Messiah. However, midway through his sermon, something shocking and unforeseen occurred:

> *'While Peter was still speaking these words, the Holy Spirit fell upon all those who heard the Word.*
>
> *And those of the circumcision who believed were astonished, because the Gift of the Holy Spirit had been poured out on the Gentiles also.*
>
> *For they heard them speak with tongues and magnify God.'* (Acts 10:44-46)

As Peter spoke prophetically concerning the person and work of the Lord Jesus, the Holy Spirit fell upon the whole audience! The moral of this story is that *prophetic proclamations precipitate spiritual outpourings of Grace and Power!* Indeed, the Prophetic Word gives rise to a floodtide of resurrection life, with the capacity to engulf entire communities, cities and nations!

Our Lord is the God who gives life to the dead, who raises up an exceeding great army from a valley of dry bones, who opens rivers in desolate heights and fountains in parched plains, who makes the wilderness a pool of water and the dry land springs of water, who transforms the wilderness into a fruitful field and causes the desert to rejoice and blossom as the rose, and who makes the barren woman to be a joyful mother of children!

Our high calling is to partner almighty God in the dissemination and administration of His resurrection life on planet earth. Let the river of life that is in your heart find expression through the words of your mouth! Prophesy healing! Preach deliverance! Proclaim revival!

May we stand in the company of those First Century Christians, who went forth and proclaimed the word everywhere, the Lord working with them, confirming the message with accompanying signs!

Chapter 5

Prophesying the Victory of the Cross

The Prophetic Word is both a tool for the building up of the Church and a weapon of spiritual warfare against the powers of darkness.

In the spiritual realm, warfare is conducted with *words*. Contrary to popular conception, angels and demons do not strike one another with laser-powered sabres, nor do they hurl one another through black holes in the galactic ceiling.

Spiritual warfare, as conducted by spiritual beings in heavenly places, is best illustrated in the dispute over the custody of Moses' body:

> *'Yet Michael the Archangel, in contending with the Devil, when he disputed about the body of Moses, dared not bring against him a reviling accusation, but said, "The Lord rebuke you!"'* (Jude 9)

Words are conveyors of authority and power, life and death, blessing and cursing. The old adage, 'Sticks and stones may break my bones, but words will never hurt me,' is actually a contravention of spiritual law. Words may not affect the body (initially), but they most certainly can penetrate the soul and make or break the spirit. Words are the most powerful medium in the universe.

For this reason, God gave the divine revelation to holy men, who, in turn, committed it to paper and ink, thereby bequeathing to the world the Bible – the Word of God that lives and abides forever.

For the same reason, God ordained that the message of salvation should be disseminated through *preaching*, and the Kingdom of God should be established through *prayer, praise* and *prophetic proclamation!*

Words are agents of spiritual authority, and as such, are central to the action of spiritual warfare. When redeemed ones give voice to the Prophetic Word of God in the power of His Spirit, demons tremble, strongholds of evil are shaken and eventually cast down, and the gates (the counsels and powers) of hell are broken.

> *'For though we walk in the flesh, we do not war according to the flesh.*
>
> *For the weapons of our warfare are not carnal but mighty in God for pulling down strongholds.*
>
> *Casting down arguments and every high thing that exalts itself against the knowledge of God, bringing every thought into captivity to the obedience of Christ.'*
>
> (2 Corinthians 10:3–5)

One of the weapons of which Paul speaks is the sword of the Prophetic Word. In his classic treatise on spiritual warfare, recorded in Ephesians chapter six, Paul describes the various pieces of armour that God has provided for Christian soldiers on active duty. Of all the equipment listed, the only offensive weapon is the *'sword of the Spirit, the word (rhema) of God.'*

The Greek word *'rhema'*, translated 'word', is the *quickened or spoken Word of God*. It is the Word that God speaks or quickens to one by His Spirit, which one then speaks forth in faith.

In this sense, 'rhema' is a *Prophetic Word*, inasmuch as it is inspired by the Spirit of God, at a specific time, for a specific purpose. 'Rhema' is the word that is *now* proceeding from the mouth of God; that which God is *now saying* concerning individuals, churches and nations.

'Rhema', the receiving and speaking forth of a word from God, is an act of spiritual warfare that greatly discomforts the enemy, and if persistently maintained, will eventually cause him to flee.

It may be the quoting of a quickened scripture, or the proclamation of a revelatory word that conforms to the benchmark of biblical truth; either way, it is the action of the 'sword of the spirit', cutting in pieces the snares of the devil!

Mountain Moving Prophecy

Christians are called upon to prophesy the victory of the Cross of Jesus, and thereby move mountains of satanic opposition that hinder and thwart the progress of God's kingdom.

When faced with a mountain, we are not to negotiate on climber's rights or seek to obtain a miner's license! Nor are we to embark on an orienteering excursion. Jesus clearly says: *'Move that mountain!'* How? *By addressing it with the word of the Lord!*

> *'For assuredly, I say to you, Whoever says to this mountain, "Be removed and be cast into the sea", and does not doubt in his heart, but believes that those things he says will come to pass, he will have whatever he says.'*
> (Mark 11:23)

Mark well: Jesus is *not* teaching the power of positive confession! Rather, He is introducing His disciples to the concept of 'rhema power' – the power that is invested in the word of the Lord and released through the proclamation of faith.

'Whoever says to this mountain...' Says what to the mountain? *Whatever God is saying to the mountain!* The sword of the Spirit is the word, quickened by the Spirit of God and proclaimed by the voice of faith.

Jesus prefaced this teaching with a practical demonstration of 'Prophetic Word power'. The previous day, en route from Bethany to Jerusalem, He had seen a fig tree afar off having leaves. Although it was not yet the season for figs, the putting forth of leaves indicated the presence of fruit.

However, a closer inspection revealed that the fig tree was lying, having nothing but leaves. In response, Jesus said to it, *'Let no one eat fruit from you ever again.'* He talked to the tree, and worse still, His disciples heard it!

Jesus then resumed His journey to Jerusalem, went into the Temple and began to drive out those who bought and sold there, overturning the tables of the money-changers in the process! In the evening the small Apostolic band returned to Bethany.

The next morning, following the same route over the Mount of Olives, the disciples saw the fig tree dried up from the roots. Peter, remembering the startling events of the previous day, said to Jesus, *'Rabbi, look! The fig tree which you cursed has withered away.'*

Jesus replied, *'Have the faith of God. For assuredly, I say to you, whoever says to this mountain...'* In other words, 'This is the work and operation of the law of faith. This is the faith of God in action. If you apply yourselves to learn the ways of faith, you will be able to live and minister in the power of God.'

Faith is released through the Prophetic Word – through the 'rhema process' of hearing and proclaiming the word of the Lord. However, we must be sure that we are speaking the word of the Lord to the mountain, and not the word of our own wishful thinking or fanciful imagination.

Unsheathe the sword of the Spirit! Proclaim the word of faith! And move that mountain clear into the sea!

> *'Fear not, you worm Jacob, you men of Israel! I will help you,' says the LORD and your Redeemer, the Holy One of Israel.*
>
> *'Behold, I will make you into a new threshing sledge with sharp teeth; you shall thresh the mountains and beat them small, and make the hills like chaff.*

You shall winnow them, the wind shall carry them away, and the whirlwind shall scatter them; you shall rejoice in the LORD, and glory in the Holy One of Israel.' (Isaiah 41:14–16)

How does the Lord turn a worm into a warrior? How does the Lord help one overcome the forces of darkness that stand in opposition to His purpose? *By putting His word in one's heart and mouth, even the word of faith, yes, even the Prophetic Word of authority and power!*

'Behold, I will make you into a new threshing sledge with sharp teeth,' the Lord says. The threshing sledge is a symbol of the Prophetic Word. Once again, we see the Spirit and the word working together to accomplish the will of God.

The *'threshing sledge'* of the Prophetic Word threshes the 'mountains' of satanic opposition and beats them small, and makes the hills like chaff. The 'wind' (Hebrew *'ruwach'*) of the Spirit then carries them away and scatters them like refuse in the sea.

Notice that God does not promise to act unilaterally and solve our problems for us. Nor does Jesus instruct us to ask the Lord to move the mountain out of the way. God helps us by putting His word in our mouth. He drives out Satan by placing the sword of the Spirit in our lips.

We must achieve a greater level of maturity by accepting a greater measure of responsibility in the Prophetic Word.

As we venture out in faith in the proclamation of prophetic truth, we will discover to our delight, that the Prophetic Word is a creative word which releases the supernatural energy of God in the circumstances of life.

Isaiah goes on to say that when the poor and needy seek water and there is none, the Lord will *open* rivers in desolate places, He will *make* the wilderness a pool of water, He will *plant* in the wilderness the cedar and the acacia tree, He will *set* in the desert the cypress tree and the pine;

'...that they may see and know, and consider

51

and understand together, that the hand of the LORD has
done this, and the Holy One of Israel has created it.'

(Isaiah 41:17–20)

Open. Make. Plant. Set. These are sovereign words of creative ability and dynamic strength.

No rhema of God is void of the power of fulfilment (Luke 1:37). Indeed, the Word that goes forth from His mouth *shall not return to Him void, but shall accomplish what He pleases and prosper in the purpose for which it is sent!* (Isaiah 55:11).

Opening Closed Doors

Inherent in the Prophetic Word is the power to open closed doors and break through satanic defences. The combined force of the Prophetic Word and the anointing of the Holy Spirit is like a battering ram that smashes through the gates of Hell!

'Thus says the LORD to His Anointed, To Cyrus, whose right hand I have held – to subdue nations before him and loose the armor of kings, to open before him the double doors, so that the gates will not be shut:

"I will go before you and make the crooked places straight; I will break in pieces the gates of bronze and cut the bars of iron.

I will give you the treasures of darkness and hidden riches of secret places, that you may know that I, the LORD, who call you by your name, am the God of Israel."'

(Isaiah 45:1–3)

The Prophetic Word conquers nations and situations – it moves in and takes charge of the *status quo*. The Prophetic Word disarms kings – it paralyses the rulers of darkness in heavenly places. The Prophetic Word opens the two leaved doors and *keeps them open* – granting access to the highest realms of authority and influence.

Moreover, the Prophetic Word makes the crooked places straight, breaks in pieces the gates of bronze and cuts the bars of iron – it deals decisively with every form of demonic power that seeks to impede the advance of God's Kingdom.

The net result is the capturing of vast hordes of wealth – *treasures of darkness and hidden riches of secret places* – which, spiritually speaking, signifies the deliverance of precious souls from the tyranny of the Evil One and their transference into the Kingdom of God's dear Son (Colossians 1:13).

In the same vein, Jesus declared that the strong man should be bound, before one seeks to enter his house and plunder his goods (Matthew 12:29). The Prophetic Word is a primary weapon with which to 'bind' or neutralize the strong man.

The proclamation of truth has a dual effect: it paralyses the enemy and cuts his power line, while at the same time setting men and women free.

Glorying in the Cross

The normal Christian life, as envisaged by our heavenly Father, is described by the Apostle Paul in 2 Corinthians 2:14;

> *'Now thanks be to God who always leads us in triumph in Christ, and through us diffuses the fragrance of His knowledge in every place.'*

The imagery used by Paul is that of a Roman triumph, celebrated by victorious generals upon their return from successful military campaigns. The General entered Rome in a chariot, preceded by the captives and spoils taken in war, and followed by his troops. In this fashion, they proceeded in state along the sacred way to the Capitol.

Accompanying the General in his chariot were his young children, and sometimes his confidential friends, while behind him stood a slave, holding over his head a jewelled crown. The body of the infantry brought up the rear, their spears adorned with laurel. Together they shouted 'Triumph!' and sang hymns of praise to the gods and to their leader.

R.F. Weymouth says of this verse: *'But to God be the thanks who in Christ ever leads us in His **triumphal procession**...'* James Moffatt says, *'Wherever I go, thank God, He makes my life **a constant pageant of triumph** in Christ...'*

Our triumph is in the Cross of the Lord Jesus. Colossians 2:15 declares that God *'disarmed principalities and powers, and made a public spectacle of them, triumphing over them in it* (the Cross).'

The Cross was the *means* of Messiah's victory over sin, death and hell. Through the Cross, He became Heaven's offering for the sins of the world. Through the Cross, He absorbed the righteous judgment of God for the conglomerate sin of mankind. Through the Cross, He cancelled the dominion of Satan and delivered man from the power of darkness. Through the Cross, He redeemed and reconciled man unto God in righteousness and true holiness!

For this reason, the Apostle Paul *'gloried'*, *'boasted'* and *'rejoiced'* in the Cross of the Lord Jesus Christ (Galatians 6:14). The Cross is the means of Messiah's victory and our redemption; therefore, it is the *focus* of the Triumph!

The Holy Spirit desires to move upon us in a strong prophetic anointing, that we might glory in the victory of the Cross ... celebrate the sacrificed Lamb of God ... and proclaim the death, burial and resurrection of our Lord with understanding and authority!

The Spirit of truth desires to reveal to us the length and breadth and height and depth of Jesus' victory over the principalities and powers of darkness. He longs to show us the dimensions of Messiah's kingdom, the universality of His dominion and the ultimacy of His power.

Moreover, the Spirit would make known the Name that is above all names, the Sceptre that is above all sceptres, and the Throne that is above all thrones, in order that we might 'boast prophetically' of the Lamb and the Cross and the Blood and the Word!

Prophetic Praise

The Book of Psalms is, in effect, the score and script of the King's Triumph. Psalm 47:1 exhorts: *'Oh, clap your hands, all you peoples! Shout to God with the **voice of triumph!'** And again, in Psalm 106:47;

> *'Save us, O LORD our God, and gather us from among the Gentiles, to give thanks to Your Holy Name, and to triumph in Your praise.'*

For the most part, the Psalms are a celebration of God's victory in the face of mountainous opposition – prophetic proclamations of daring faith in the very teeth of the adversary!

Many of David's offerings of praise and thanksgiving were made *before the event* of deliverance, in anticipation of God's ultimate victory. David praised the Lord and made prophetic proclamations of triumph while Saul was still pursuing him, while his life was still in danger, while he was still being mocked, rejected and persecuted.

Yet it was these very proclamations, made upon the basis of God's covenantal faithfulness and lovingkindness, that turned the tables on the powers of darkness, overthrew their malicious schemes, and brought David through to personal victory.

Christians of the twentieth century have the luxury of looking back almost 2,000 years to the death of Jesus on the Cross, and of realizing that victory has been established once and for all over the powers of darkness, and that deliverance has been eternally secured!

However, this does not mean that all our problems will automatically disappear, nor does it mean that the enemy will avoid contesting our liberty in Christ.

The Devil will not flee until he is confronted with the truth of Jesus' victory and his defeat; He will not yield an inch unless he is expelled by the administration of Jesus' authority.

Consequently, we must go into all the world (every

sphere of life) and proclaim the gospel (the victory of the Cross). The result? People will be saved, lives will be changed, and demons will be driven out! (Mark 16:15–18)

The prophetic proclamation of the victory of the Cross is one of the most powerful weapons in the Christian armament. Indeed, it is destined to play an increasingly decisive role in the Church's assault on the strongholds of evil in the last days:

> *'Then I heard a loud voice saying in Heaven, "Now salvation, and strength, and the Kingdom of our God, and the power of His Christ have come, for the accuser of our brethren, who accused them before our God day and night, has been cast down.*
>
> *And they overcame him by the Blood of the Lamb and by the word of their testimony, and they did not love their lives to the death."'* (Revelation 12:10, 11)

The blood of the Lamb (the victory of the Cross) and the word of our testimony: A winning combination in heaven and on earth!

Chapter 6

Prophesying the Course of History

Messiah Jesus is Lord, not only of the Church, but also of history. He is the Lamb upon the Throne, who takes the scroll of redemption and opens its seals. All of the end-time purposes and judgments of God, including the emergence of the antichrist and his 'New World Order', are under the full control of the Son of God!

The Lord Jesus controls the destiny of men and nations, indeed, the destiny of the earth and all its fullness. In the beginning He laid the foundation of the earth and fashioned the heavens with His hands. On an appointed day He will fold them up like a cloak, cast them into the fire, and bring forth new heavens and a new earth, free from the contamination of sin, sickness and death! (Hebrews 1:10–12; 2 Peter 3:12, 13).

The Sovereign Lord – the grand Architect of history – determined the allotted periods of the nations, giving to them the cycles they were to pass through and fixing a time for their rise and fall. Moreover, He marked out the boundaries of their habitations, assigning to each nation its territorial rights (Acts 17:26).

He changes the times and the seasons; He removes kings and raises up kings; He rules in the kingdom of men, and gives it to whomever He will (Daniel 2:21; 4:17). He does according to His will in the army of heaven and among the inhabitants of the earth. No one can restrain His hand or say to Him, 'What have you done?' (Daniel 5:35).

Jesus is the King of the nations – the Potter who holds the nations in His hands like lumps of clay, making them or breaking them according to His will (Jeremiah 10:7; 18:6–10). He is the Lord of heaven, who holds men's breath in His hand and owns all their ways (Daniel 5:23).

All things were created through the Lord Jesus and for His glory. He is the *centre* in which the universe coheres! He is the *source*, He is the *means*, and He is the *end*. *Of* Him, and *through* Him, and *to* Him are all things! (Colossians 1:16, 17).

The Lord Jesus possesses all authority in heaven and on earth (Matthew 28:18). He is seated at the right hand of Father God, high above all other government and authority and power and dominion, and any title of sovereignty that can be named (Ephesians 1:21). At His Name every knee shall bow, in heaven, on earth, and under the earth, and to His lordship every tongue shall confess (Philippians 2:10).

In light of the exalted position of the Son of God, and the supremacy of His nature and power, it behoves us to understand how He exercises authority in the affairs of men and shapes the course of world history.

The King's Sceptre

Almighty God rules by decree throughout His universal Kingdom. Indeed, the Word of God is the most powerful force in the universe; the final authority in heaven and earth!

The Creator-Son upholds all things by the word of His power (Hebrews 1:3), or as the Amplified Bible puts it, *'upholds and maintains and guides and propels the universe by His mighty word of power.'*

The Greek word *'rhema'*, translated 'word', is used sixty-seven times in the New Testament, and primarily denotes *the spoken word*.

Jesus rules by the word that proceeds from His mouth. During His three and one-half years of earthly ministry, Jesus exercised authority and changed the course of history with His tongue! He forgave sin, healed the sick, cast out demons, raised the dead, stilled the raging storm, multiplied food, executed judgment and bestowed blessing *with words!*

The book of Revelation describes the closing stages of human history, with Jesus rising forth from Heaven on a white horse as King of kings and Lord of lords. Out of His mouth goes a sharp sword with which He disciplines the nations (Revelation 19:15). That sword is the Prophetic Word of God, proclaimed through the power of the Holy Spirit!

Before and after, Jesus rules by the Prophetic Word. But what about now? Jesus is often referred to as the 'soon coming King'. That He is coming soon, there is no doubt. However, He is not coming *to be* King; He is already King! *Now* He is Lord of the nations and Ruler of the kings of the earth!

Psalm 110 speaks of the exaltation of Messiah, a prophecy that was fulfilled in the resurrection and ascension of the Lord Jesus:

'*The* LORD *said to my Lord, "Sit at My right hand, till I make Your enemies Your footstool."*

The LORD *shall send the rod of Your strength out of Zion. Rule in the midst of Your enemies!*

Your people shall be volunteers in the day of Your power; in the beauties of holiness, from the womb of the morning, You have the dew of Your youth.

The LORD *has sworn and will not relent, "You are a priest forever according to the order of Melchizedek."*

The Lord is at Your right hand; He shall execute kings in the day of His wrath.

He shall judge among the nations, He shall fill the places with dead bodies, He shall execute the heads of many countries.

He shall drink of the brook by the wayside; therefore He shall lift up the head.'

'The LORD', Yahweh – God the Father, said to 'my Lord', Jesus the Messiah, *'Sit at My right hand **until I make** Your enemies Your footstool.'* We are living in 'The Great Until'.

Jesus said, *'All authority has been given to Me in heaven and **on earth**.'* Right now, as you read these words, Messiah is ruling from Heaven and directing the course of history from the Throne of God!

If Jesus is in heaven, how does He rule in the midst of His enemies on earth? *Through His Body, the Church! 'The Lord shall send the rod of Your strength out of Zion.'*

'Zion' is an actual hill in Jerusalem, renowned as the site of David's Tabernacle and the home of the Ark of the Covenant. However, in spiritual terms, 'Zion' encompasses more than just a geographical location in the Middle East.

'Zion' speaks of God's dwelling place on earth; the site of His throne, the seat of His Government, and the habitation of His presence. 'Zion' is, above all else, a place of praise and worship – God in the midst of His people, manifesting His presence, demonstrating His power and revealing His glory.

In spiritual terms, 'Zion' is wherever two or three are gathered together in the Name of Jesus to worship the Lord. 'Zion' is the living Body of Messiah, the members of which are built together to form a spiritual house and a holy temple, a habitation of God in the Spirit! (Ephesians 2:21, 22)

The Lord Jesus rules from Heaven, through His Church on earth, by the rod of His strength. The Hebrew word *'matteh'*, as used in this context, denotes *a king's sceptre*. J.B. Rotherham translates this verse: *'Thy sceptre of strength will Yahweh extend out of Zion.'*

What is the sceptre of Messiah? The Prophetic Word that issues from His lips! The prophet Isaiah said of Jesus, *'He shall strike the earth with **the rod of His mouth**, and with the breath of His lips He shall slay the wicked'* (Isaiah 11:4).

The Prophetic Word is the voice of Jesus, speaking from heaven, intervening and over-ruling in the affairs of men.

Through that word He judges among the nations; He changes the times and the seasons; He removes kings and raises up kings; He *'breaks in pieces'* the heads of many countries; He dethrones principalities and powers; and He alters the spiritual status quo in the heavens.

But in order for Jesus to effectively rule by the sceptre of the Prophetic Word, His people must be willing, or free-will offerings, or spontaneous volunteers in the day of His power. They must be willing to prophesy, willing to praise, and willing to pray; willing to be a voice for the Prophetic Word; willing, if necessary, to proclaim in the wilderness the way of the Lord!

The sovereignty of the Prophetic Word is aptly portrayed in this re-occurring biblical phrase: *'That it might be fulfilled which was spoken by the Lord through the mouth of the prophet...'* Clearly, the flow of history is regulated by the Prophetic Word of God.

For this reason, *'The Lord God does nothing without first revealing His secret to His servants the prophets'* (Amos 3:7). It is the prophet's responsibility to lift up the word of the Lord in prayer, praise and prophetic proclamation! *'He who has My Word, let him speak My Word faithfully'* (Jeremiah 23:28).

With every genuine prophetic utterance, there is a stretching forth of the King's sceptre – a release of His power and authority in the earth – that changes the circumstances of life and the destiny of nations!

He Spoke and it Was Done

To effectively co-labour with the Lord, one must understand the unique way in which He brings His Kingdom purposes to pass on planet earth. God's ways are perfectly consistent, from Genesis through to Revelation. On almost every page of the Bible, one sees God *speaking* and *acting*, in that order!

God's way of working is recorded by David in Psalm thirty-three:

> *'For the word of the LORD is right, and all His work is done in truth.*
>
> *By the Word of the LORD the heavens were made, and all the host of them by the breath of His mouth.*
>
> *For He spoke, and it was done; He commanded, and it stood fast.'* (Psalm 33:4, 6, 9)

Notice that God's *Word* precedes His *Work*. God *speaks*, and then it is *done*; He *commands*, and then it *stands fast*. The word of the Lord creates, initiates, sets in order, and maintains.

The way of the Lord is revealed in the first chapter of the Bible, as almighty God sets about creating the heavens and the earth. God said, *'Light be,'* and light was! God said, *'Let an expanse be in the midst of the waters,'* and it was so!

Eleven times it is written, *'And God said...'* Through repetition, the Word of God is trying to teach us something of the ways of God. God speaks and it is done.

This puts prayer, praise and prophecy in a different light. All of a sudden, the spoken word assumes new significance. True 'prayer in the Spirit' is prayer that originates in the heart of God, prayer that is according to His will, and prayer that is inspired and guided by the Holy Spirit. The same is true of praise and prophecy.

Prayer, praise or prophecy 'in the Spirit', is the speaking of God's words back to Him – becoming a voice for the word of the Lord in the earth. When the priests and Levites came to question John the Baptist's credentials, he replied, *'I am a voice...'* The Word is God's, the voice is ours. But when God's word and man's voice combine, there is a manifestation of the Kingdom and a performance of the will of God on earth, just as in heaven!

Why is it imperative that the Lord should find a voice for His word in the earth? Because God's will cannot be *done* until it is first *spoken!*

In the beginning, the Lord committed the stewardship of the earth into the hands of man (Genesis 1:26–28). In so doing, He deliberately bound Himself to work *with* and *through* man to accomplish His purposes in the world.

As far as the earth is concerned, God cannot work unilaterally – not because He lacks the power, but because He has legally committed Himself to the agency of man. To bypass man would be to violate His own laws of justice.

This explains why God is continually searching for people to stand before Him in the place of intercession; people who will wait on the Lord and receive the knowledge of His will; people who, having received the revelation, will lift up their voices in prayer, praise and prophetic utterance (Ezekiel 22:30).

Indeed, the eyes of the Lord run to and fro throughout the whole earth, searching for those whose hearts are loyal to Him, whom He can trust, and in whose mouths He can put His Word.

> *'Then the LORD put forth His hand and touched my mouth, and the LORD said to me: "Behold, I have put My words in your mouth.*
> *See, I have this day set you over the nations and over the kingdoms, to root out and to pull down, to destroy and to throw down, to build and to plant."'*
>
> (Jeremiah 1:9, 10)

This scripture captures the essence of prophetic utterance and ministry: God placing His hand upon one's life and putting His Word in one's mouth. The effect of the Word is to 'root out, pull down, destroy, throw down' and to 'build and plant'.

In other words, to set God's purpose in motion among the nations; to facilitate the fulfilment of God's will on earth, according to the pattern that is established in Heaven.

May we be the generation of which the Psalmist spoke:

> *'The LORD gave the Word; great was the company of those who proclaimed it!'* (Psalm 68:11)

Chapter 7

Prophesying, Praising and Praying

Wednesday, 7.30pm – Prayer Meeting.

Notices such as these are standard fare in church bulletins all over the world. What is your first impression upon reading the words, 'Prayer Meeting'. A thrill of joyous anticipation, or dreary resignation?

What scene passes through your mind as you contemplate personal attendance: A handful of little old ladies occupying the front rows of a near-deserted building; an hour of spiritual gloom as prayer warriors faithfully inform God of besetting needs, depressing detail by depressing detail?

Regretfully, these intuitive expectations are too often realized in the average church prayer meeting. The reason? Most prayer originates in the soul, not the spirit; it proceeds from the mind of man rather than the heart of God.

God's Word exhorts us to *'pray ... at all times ... in the Spirit!'* There is a world of difference between mere prayer, and *'praying in the Spirit.'*

It is not unusual for people, in a time of conscious need, to petition a 'Higher Power'. Unregenerate hearts around the world are constantly being lifted up in prayer to real or imagined beings, who, it is hoped, will intercede with grace and power to alleviate human suffering.

There is nothing special about prayer. A popular text in many a Christian home states that 'prayer changes things'.

However, this is not entirely true. Prayer, of itself, changes nothing. But when that prayer is born of the Spirit, empowered by the Spirit and offered in the Spirit, it changes everything!

For prayer to be effective, it must connect with the power of God. And for prayer to connect with the power of God, it must proceed from the Spirit. *'Out of your innermost being shall flow rivers of living water'* (John 7:38).

Following this theme, the Psalmist exhorts: *'Trust in Him at all times, you people; pour out your heart before Him'* (Psalm 62:8). Notice that he says, *'Pour out your heart,'* and not, 'Pour out your head!'

However, personal experience testifies that many prayer meetings degenerate into outpourings of people's heads: natural-minded prayers that tell God of the problem and advise Him of an appropriate course of action!

The three ground rules of effective, spiritual prayer are 'Look, Listen and Learn.' *Look* to see what God is showing you, *listen* to hear what God is saying to you, and *learn* how you should pray. This kind of preparation makes for real prophetic praying, that touches the throne of God and changes human lives!

We would do well to heed the words of the Apostle James when it comes to prayer: *'Let every man be swift to hear, slow to speak, slow to wrath'* (James 1:19). Swift to hear what the Spirit is saying, and slow to speak out our own preconceptions (or misconceptions as the case may be).

Thanks to the grace of God, I am learning to defer to the leadership of the Holy Spirit in prayer. Before entering into prayer, I wait on the prophetic anointing of the Spirit. I begin to praise and thank the Lord, and sing in the Spirit.

As the Holy Spirit rises up on the inside, there comes a manifestation of His presence, and with His presence there comes a revelation of God's will and purpose.

The first epistle of John contains an iron-clad guarantee of answered prayer:

'Now this is the confidence that we have in Him, that if we ask anything according to His will, He hears us.

And if we know that He hears us, whatever we ask, we know that we have the petitions that we have asked of Him.' (1 John 5:14, 15)

Consider the following prayer equation: To be heard by God, one must pray according to His will; to pray according to His will, one must pray *prophetically*. To pray prophetically, one must pray by *revelation*; to pray by revelation, one must pray *in the Spirit*.

Prophetic prayer, therefore, is prayer that originates in the heart and mind of God (prayer that is according to His will), the theme and content of which is revealed to one's spirit-man by the Spirit of God, which prayer is subsequently lifted up to the Throne of God in waves of Holy Spirit-empowered utterance.

Words That the Holy Spirit Teaches

The need for prophetic revelation of the Spirit in prayer is demonstrated in the eighth chapter of the book of Romans:

'Likewise the Spirit also helps in our weaknesses. For we do not know what we should pray for as we ought, but the Spirit Himself makes intercession for us with groanings which cannot be uttered.

Now He who searches the hearts knows what the mind of the Spirit is, because He makes intercession for the saints according to the will of God.'

(Romans 8:26, 27)

The Greek word *'astheneia'*, translated 'weaknesses', denotes *the limitations and inadequacies of the natural man.* According to W.E. Vine, *'astheneia'* indicates *an inability to produce results.*

The weakness or inability here spoken of is our limitation

and inadequacy in *prayer*. We do not know what we should pray for, nor how to pray for it, as we ought!

In his first epistle to the Corinthians, Paul elaborates on this weakness:

> *'But as it is written: "Eye has not seen, nor ear heard, nor have entered into the heart of man the things which God has prepared for those who love Him."*
>
> *But the natural man does not receive the things of the Spirit of God, for they are foolishness to him; nor can he know them, because they are spiritually discerned.'*
>
> (1 Corinthians 2:9, 14)

Natural man is carnal, or 'sense-ruled'. He derives the majority of his knowledge from the five physical senses: seeing, hearing, touching, tasting and smelling.

However, the 'deep things of God' – those things that pertain to His eternal will and purpose – cannot be perceived through the gateway of the senses. God is a Spirit, and He communicates His deepest truths to spirits. *'Deep calls unto deep'* (Psalm 42:7). Thus, natural man has very limited access to the knowledge of God.

For this reason, the Bible calls the will and purpose of God a 'mystery', inasmuch as it is outside the range of natural apprehension and can only be known by divine revelation.

How often do we find ourselves praying out of 'weakness' or natural inadequacy! Like Peter on the Mount of Transfiguration, we don't know what to say, so we just go ahead and say it anyway!

Praying out of a natural mind limits faith and nullifies the operation of the Holy Spirit. However, prophetic praying – praying out of a revelation of the mind of God – releases faith and looses the power of the Holy Spirit to work on man's behalf!

How does one enter into the knowledge of the things that God has prepared for those who love Him? Once again, the Apostle Paul provides the answer:

'But God has revealed them to us through His Spirit. For the Spirit searches all things, yes, the deep things of God.' (1 Corinthians 2:10)

God reveals the knowledge of His will and purpose through the Person of the Holy Spirit. Paul goes on to say that the very reason for which we have received the Holy Spirit is that we might know the things that have been freely given to us by God!

The Lord Jesus enjoyed a closer relationship with the Holy Spirit than any other man in history. He demonstrated the Spirit's power and proved the Spirit's faithfulness. Speaking to His disciples out of personal experience, Jesus said, *'When He, the Truth-giving Spirit, has come, He will guide you into all Truth ... He will tell you things to come ... He will teach you all things'* (John 14:26, 16:13).

The Holy Spirit helps us overcome the limitations of our humanity by searching out the deep things of God and declaring unto us that which He sees and hears. This is especially true in respect to prayer.

It is the Spirit who prompts us to pray in the first place. As we obey His prompting and wait upon His leading, He comes to our aid with the right kind of prayer for that particular moment of time.

The Spirit helps by making intercession *for* us and *through* us with groanings that cannot be uttered in human vocabulary, which intercession is in perfect harmony with the will of God. Indeed, the Spirit's intercession is the vocal expression of the heart and mind of God for His children!

'Sunantilambano', translated 'helps' in Romans 8:26, is a very interesting Greek compound. It is made up of *'sun'* (together with), *'anti'* (over against) and *'lambano'* (to take).

The word speaks of *the action of a person coming to another's aid by taking hold over against that person, of the load he is carrying.* The person helping does not take the whole load, but helps the other person in his endeavour.

Notice carefully that the Holy Spirit does not assume the

whole load of prayer; rather, He takes hold together with us in our prayer endeavour. The notion that the Holy Spirit does all the work is one of the main reasons why some people never speak in tongues.

Before I pray for people to receive the Baptism of the Holy Spirit, I get them to read Acts 2:4 aloud, and then ask him, 'Who did the speaking?'

'The Holy Spirit,' they reply. So I say, 'Read it again.' We repeat this process until they finally come up with the right answer. According to Acts 2:4, it was the disciples who spoke in tongues, and it was the Holy Spirit who gave them utterance (ability and inspiration).

The Holy Spirit does not do it alone. It is essential that people get this simple truth clear in their minds, otherwise they just sit there like stuffed dummies, waiting for something to happen!

The Holy Spirit will take hold together with us, but He needs the co-operation of our spirit, mind and body. He will give us the prayer to pray and the song to sing, but we must do the praying and the singing! He will lead us into new depths of prayer and new heights of praise, but we must consecrate our voice for His use.

> *'Now we have received, not the spirit of the world, but the Spirit who is from God, that we might know the things that have been freely given to us by God.*
>
> *These things we also speak, not in words which man's wisdom teaches but which the Holy Spirit teaches, comparing spiritual things with spiritual.'*
>
> (1 Corinthians 2:12, 13)

Spiritual law states that *revelation issues in proclamation*. 'We have received the Spirit who is from God, that we might know the deep things of God, which things we also speak in words that the Holy Spirit teaches.'

The revelation of the Holy Spirit overflows in prophetic prayer, praise and proclamation! Writing to the Church at Ephesus, Paul said: *'Be filled with the Spirit, **speaking** to one*

*another in psalms and hymns and spiritual songs, **singing**
and making melody in your heart to the Lord'* (Ephesians
5:18, 19).

The revelatory anointing of the Spirit causes us to burst
forth in anthems of prophetic praise and torrents of prophetic prayer – utterances of supernatural origin, in accordance
with the will and purpose of almighty God!

A New Song

The Scriptures exhort us to *'**sing** to the Lord a new song . . .
bless His Name . . . **proclaim** the good news of His salvation
from day to day . . . **declare** His glory among the nations . . .
give to the Lord glory and strength . . . **ascribe** to the Lord the
glory due His Name . . . **bring** an offering and **come** into His
courts . . . **worship** the Lord in the beauty of holiness . . .
tremble before Him . . . **say** among the nations, "The Lord
reigns . . . "'* (Psalm 96).

The Lord is great and greatly to be praised. In other
words, the revealed greatness of God summons a commen-
surate measure of praise. A great God deserves great
praise. But whether we like to admit it or not, our praise is
proportionate to our revelation of God. Little or no revelation brings forth little or no praise!

How can we do justice to the greatness of God? How can
we possibly give to Him the glory due His Name? If we try to
praise out of our own strength and understanding, we will
surely fail. As with prayer, we need the Holy Spirit to come
alongside and take hold together with us in the ministry of
praise.

> *'And do not be drunk with wine, in which is dissipation;
> but be filled with the Spirit,*
>
> *speaking to one another in psalms and hymns and
> spiritual songs, singing and making melody in your
> heart to the Lord,*
>
> *giving thanks always for all things to God the Father
> in the Name of our Lord Jesus Christ.'*
>
> (Ephesians 5:18–20)

How can we offer appropriate praise to the living God? *Be filled with the Spirit!* How can we proclaim the good news of His salvation; how can we declare His glory; how can we announce His Kingdom? *Be filled with the Spirit!* The Spirit is the source, the inspiration, the energy and the understanding!

It's time that we learned to praise out of the river of life within us. Don't praise out of your feelings. Don't praise out of your natural mind. Praise from the heart. Praise out of the anointing of the Holy Spirit.

The Holy Spirit is the conductor of Heaven's orchestra and Earth's choir; the director of universal praise and worship of the Lamb; the master of song; executive composer and producer, all rolled into one.

'Sing to the Lord a new song...' The new song of which the Bible speaks is more than a newly composed chorus or a recently learned hymn. It is a prophetic song that expresses the heart and mind of God at a given moment of time.

The new song is a song of prophetic revelation concerning the person and work of the Lord Jesus; a prophetic celebration of the redemption of Messiah:

> *'Oh, sing to the Lord a new song! For He has done marvellous things; His right hand and His holy arm have gained Him the victory.*
>
> *The Lord has made known His salvation; His righteousness He has openly shown in the sight of the nations.*
>
> *He has remembered His mercy and His faithfulness to the house of Israel; all the ends of the earth have seen the salvation of our God.'* (Psalm 98:1–3)

The new song is a product of the inspiration of the Holy Spirit, a fruit of revelation knowledge, and a response to the vision of the glory of the Lord.

In the fifth chapter of the book of Revelation, John describes a scene from heaven's throne-room. A universal search is being conducted for a worthy redeemer who can open the scroll and loose its seals. John weeps profusely when the search fails to yield a qualified candidate.

Then suddenly, One appears in the midst of the throne: a freshly slain Lamb, dead and yet alive again, with seven horns and seven eyes. Boldly He approaches the throne to take the scroll out of the right hand of God the Father!

Upon the revelation of the Lamb as redeemer, the four Living Creatures and the twenty-four Elders fall down in worship, each having a harp, and golden bowls full of incense, which are the prayers of the saints.

> *'And they sang a new song, saying: "You are worthy to take the scroll, and to open its seals; for You were slain, and have redeemed us to God by Your blood out of every tribe and tongue and people and nation,*
>
> *And have make us kings and priests to our God; and we shall reign on the earth."'* (Revelation 5:9, 10)

The new song is the result of standing before the throne and receiving a revelation of the great Lamb-Messiah-Redeemer. One cannot help but fall down and let the rivers of praise and worship flow forth from one's innermost being!

The Fear of the Lord

Prophetic praise and worship, or the singing of the new song, releases something in the invisible realm that bears rich fruit in the natural, seen world. King David said:

> *'He has put a new song in my mouth – praise to our God; many will see it and fear, and will trust in the* LORD.' (Psalm 40:3)

That 'something' is called *the Fear of the Lord!* The new song releases the power of the Holy Spirit to change lives, heal sick bodies, restore broken marriages and expel demonic personalities!

The new song catalyses the manifestation of God's holy presence. *'You are holy, who inhabit the praises of Israel.'* Some of today's most outstanding miracles are taking place right in the midst of praise and worship services – without the laying on of hands, the anointing of oil, or the prayer of faith!

God is sovereignly moving by His Spirit, showing Himself strong on behalf of those whose hearts are lifted up to Him in true spiritual worship! Indeed, it is a good thing to give thanks unto the Lord and to sing praises to His Name!

If this is happening in homes and churches, can you imagine what will happen when the choir-army of the Lord takes to the streets and fills our towns and cities with the praises of the Lord and the music of Heaven!

Evil principalities and powers will be bound and cast down; spiritual atmospheres will be transformed; modern-day Pharaohs will be confronted and humbled, and multitudes will be set free to worship the true and living God. God's power will sweep like a whirlwind through the land!

New Praise for a New Day

The spontaneity of Spirit-inspired prophetic praise is depicted in the Levitical ministry of David's Tabernacle.

David was a psalmist, a prophet, and a king, in that order. He envisaged the death, resurrection and eternal kingdom of the Messiah in word and song. His own life, lived out in the power of the Spirit, foreshadowed a new and everlasting covenant, based upon better promises.

The Tabernacle of David introduced Israel to a new order of praise and worship, that, in many ways, prefigured the Melchizedek priesthood of the New Covenant.

David instituted a continuous ministry of praise and worship before the Ark of the Lord, complete with stringed instruments, harps, cymbals and trumpets! For some Levites, their whole responsibility was to minister to the Lord in celebration, thanksgiving and praise (1 Chronicles. 16:4).

Another feature of this ministry was the singing or chanting of psalms, hymns and spiritual songs, something unheard of in the days of Moses' Tabernacle. The prophetic and spontaneous nature of these spiritual sacrifices should not be underestimated. Indeed, holy men of God spoke and sang as they were moved by the Spirit! (2 Peter 1:21)

> *'So he left Asaph and his brothers there before the Ark of the Covenant of the* LORD *to minister before the Ark regularly, as every day's work required.'*
> (1 Chronicles 16:37)

The above quoted scripture contains one of the most powerful principles of prayer and worship in the Bible! Notice carefully the last five words: *'To minister before the Ark regularly, **as every day's work required.'***

Personally speaking, I do not like set structures of prayer and praise. I have never found such regimented approaches conducive to moving in the Spirit.

There are certain basic guide-lines that one should follow in prayer and worship. I find it helpful to read a portion of the Word, pray or sing in the Spirit, and praise the Lord. Sometimes I will read and then sing, other times I will intersperse reading with singing.

But the bottom line is this: *once I get into the Spirit, I allow the Holy Spirit to take the lead*. I just follow His directions. Whether I cover all my prepared prayer points or not, is of little importance. After all, the Holy Spirit knows the will of God perfectly; He knows exactly *'what each day's work requires.'*

To my mind, this is the most effective way of praying and praising. It is, as Paul said, *'Praying at all times with all kinds of prayer in the power of the Spirit'* (Ephesians 6:18).

The Holy Spirit knows precisely what kind of prayer and praise is required for today. And most likely, it will be a different kind of prayer and praise than that which was offered up yesterday!

One should never underestimate the variety and

creativity of the Holy Spirit in praying and praising. *'There are various kinds of gifts, but the same Spirit'* (1 Corinthians 12:4).

It is the leadership of the Spirit that makes our praying and praising *prophetic!* The Spirit has a new prayer for a new season and a new praise for a new day! Remember, God 'puts' the new song in our mouth; we don't manufacture it in our own strength and wisdom.

Prophetic praise is the praise created by the Spirit of God. In the book of Isaiah, the Lord says: *'I create the fruit of the lips'* (Isaiah 57:19). The writer to the Hebrews borrows this phrase and expounds upon it in a New Covenant context:

> *'Therefore by Him let us continually offer the sacrifice of praise to God, that is, the fruit of our lips, giving thanks to His Name.'* (Hebrews 13:15)

The created fruit of Isaiah is the created praise of Hebrews – joyful confessions to the Name of the Lord Jesus!

To us today, as to Israel of old, the Lord says:

> **'Open your mouth wide,
> and I will fill it with My praise!'**

Chapter 8

Prophesying and Acting

The Bible refers to the period immediately preceding the return of the Lord as *'the time of the end.'* The book of Daniel contains a very interesting description of *'the time of the end,'* as given to the prophet by the arch-angel Gabriel.

> *'But you, Daniel, shut up the words, and seal the book until the time of the end; many shall run to and fro, and knowledge shall increase.'* (Daniel 12:4)

'The time of the end' is thus predicted to be a period of unprecedented prophetic revelation in which the Word of God will be read more widely and understood more thoroughly than ever before!

Almighty God, who controls the four winds of heaven, appoints times and seasons of prophetic revelation for the restoration of biblical truth to the Church. Paul alludes to this principle in Ephesians chapter three, when he writes of his knowledge in the mystery of Christ:

> *'Which in other ages was not made known to the sons of men as it has now been revealed by the Spirit to His holy apostles and prophets.'* (Ephesians 3:5)

Likewise, Daniel states that the Lord God *'changes the times and the seasons,'* and that *'He gives wisdom to the wise and knowledge to those who have understanding, and reveals deep and secret things...'* (Daniel 2:21, 22). Fresh revelation is contiguous with a change of season, or a new time frame.

In the time of revelation, *'many shall run to and fro, and knowledge shall increase.'* Revelation knowledge begets action, *prophetic action!*

'To him who knows to do good, and does not do it, to him it is sin' (James 4:17). With knowledge comes the attendant responsibility of action: *'To him who knows to do ... and does not do ... it is sin.'*

The sons of Issachar were a prophetic breed of men who had understanding of the times in which they lived. This understanding was translated into decisive action: *'To know what Israel ought to do'* (1 Chronicles 12:32).

There is a world of difference between *action* and *prophetic action*. Action is a product of the soul – the mind, will and emotions of the natural man – while prophetic action is a product of the spirit – the mind, will and emotions of Almighty God, as revealed by the indwelling Holy Spirit.

Human action rarely achieves the desired spiritual result: *'The wrath of man does not produce the righteousness of God'* (James 1:20), whereas prophetic action is guaranteed divine success: *'He who does the will of God abides forever'* (1 John 2:17).

Prophetic action springs from prophetic revelation – intimate intercourse with the Lord in prayer and worship. In such times of communion, the Lord reveals His *heart* (nature and character), and His *mind* (will and purpose) to those who worship Him in spirit and in truth.

> *'... the people who know their God will display strength and take action.'* (Daniel 11:32, NASB)

The Hebrew word *'yada'*, translated 'know', is often used to denote life's most intimate acquaintances. Of Moses it is said that the Lord *knew* Him by name and face to face (Exodus 33:17; Deuteronomy 34:10). David said, *'O LORD, You have searched me and known me, You know my sitting down and my rising up'* (Psalm 139:1, 2).

'*Yada*' is used for sexual intercourse on the part of both men and women in the well-known euphemism '*Adam knew Eve his wife,*' and its parallels (Genesis 4:1). '*Yada*' is also used to describe man's relationship to God. Israel was exhorted '*to **know**, to pursue the **knowledge** of the Lord*' (Hosea 6:3).

In the mutual sharing of love, secrets of the heart are revealed, desires are whispered, joys and sorrows are expressed – the deepest thoughts and feelings of life are divulged. This holds true, both on the horizontal level in marriage and friendship, and on the vertical level in communion with the Lord God.

Expounding upon this theme in the New Testament, Jesus said:

> *'I am the vine, you are the branches. He who abides in Me, and I in him, bears much fruit; for without Me you can do nothing.*
>
> *If you abide in Me, and My words abide in you, you will ask what you desire, and it shall be done for you.'*
>
> (John 15:5, 7)

Abiding in Jesus, two becoming one, the intimate communion of God and man in prayer and worship – such is the requisite for fruitful prophetic action ... action that stems from the heart and mind of God ... action that is in accordance with His will and purpose!

'*If you abide in Me,*' Jesus said, '*My Words will abide in you.*' My *Rhemas*. My *prophetic utterances*. And upon the foundation of the revealed word, you will *speak* and *act* and bear much fruit, that My Father may be glorified!

Acts of Faith and Power

The Bible is packed full of prophetic action. Hebrews chapter eleven is a sampler of men and women who knew God intimately and performed great exploits in His Name.

To know God is to be made strong. David said, '*The*

LORD *is the strength of my life,'* and *'The* LORD *will give strength to His people'* (Psalm 27:1, 29:11). To commune with God in the secret place, to dwell in His Holy Presence, is to be endued with power from on High.

Such power issues in *acts* of prophetic significance. It is no coincidence that the longest book in the New Testament, the book of Acts, is precisely what its name implies: *A book of Acts!*

> *'And in these days prophets came from Jerusalem to Antioch.*
>
> *Then one of them, named Agabus, stood up and showed by the Spirit that there was going to be a great famine throughout all the world, which also happened in the days of Claudius Caesar.*
>
> *Then the disciples, each according to his ability, determined to send relief to the brethren dwelling in Judea.*
>
> *This they also did, and sent it to the elders by the hands of Barnabas and Saul.'*   (Acts 11:27–30)

This is an excellent example of prophecy giving birth to practical and decisive *action*. God did not disclose the knowledge of the coming famine to the church, just so they could sit on their hands and discuss it. He gave them advance warning so that they could do something about it!

The gift of prophecy is intensely practical! Some people are shocked to realize that God actually expects them to *do what He says* in the Prophetic Word!

Human nature has the uncanny knack of growing accustomed to the most supernatural of manifestations. It is all too easy to treat the Prophetic Word as some abstract theological prose, and fail to take it seriously as a word that is to be acted upon at all costs!

The more mature the prophecy, the more practical will be its application. Vagueness is not synonymous with spirituality! God addresses people at their point of need, not with religious clichés or nebulous theories, but with clearcut instructions concerning the pathway of life.

Acting upon the Prophetic Word of the Lord commands divine favour and success; it may also save your life! A case in point is the situation of the Jewish believers in and around Jerusalem at the time of the Roman siege.

Sitting on the Mount of Olives with His disciples during the week of His passion, the Lord Jesus uttered a prophecy concerning the destruction of Jerusalem, the dispersion of the Jewish people, and the eventual restoration of the nation – a prophecy remarkable in both accuracy and detail.

> *'But when you see Jerusalem surrounded by armies, then know that its desolation is near.*
>
> *Then let those in Judea flee to the mountains, let not those who are in the country enter her.*
>
> *For these are the days of vengeance, that all things which are written may be fulfilled.*
>
> *But woe to those who are pregnant and to those who are nursing babies in those days! For there will be great distress in the land and wrath upon this people.*
>
> *And they will fall by the edge of the sword, and be led away captive into all nations. And Jerusalem will be trampled by Gentiles until the times of the Gentiles are fulfilled.'* (Luke 21:20–24)

Less than forty years later, Jesus' terrible prophecy was fulfilled, word for word, by the forces of the Roman Empire.

The Holy City had already received two reprieves. Cestius Gallus, the Roman Procurator in Syria, withdrew suddenly in October of 67 AD, when the city was his for the taking. Nine months later, upon hearing of Nero's death, Vespasian halted his march on Jerusalem and returned to Rome, to eventually be crowned as Emperor.

During the next eighteen months, those who remembered and believed the words of Jesus, fled from the city and took refuge in Pella, east of the Jordan River.

But the reprieve was short-lived, the siege was resumed,

and on May 10th, 70 AD, the shadow of Titus, Vespasian's son, fell across the walls of Jerusalem. It took Titus' army of sixty-five thousand men, 139 days to gain control of the whole city, during which time it was spared no form of savagery or horror.

Over one million people had come up to Jerusalem for the Feast of Unleavened Bread, only to find themselves shut up within the walls by the Roman siege.

Those who did not die at the hands of rival Jewish factions, starved to death by the thousands. Others who tried to escape were captured by the Romans and executed. At one stage, five hundred Jews were crucified daily within sight of those on the walls, until there was no more room to erect crosses and no more wood could be found for bodies.

Finally, on the 10th day of Ab, 70 AD (the very same day on which Solomon's Temple had been destroyed by the King of Babylon in 586 BC), the Temple was set on fire and destroyed by Roman soldiers.

The Jewish historian, Flavius Josephus, puts the final casualty figure for this siege of Jerusalem at 1,100,000. Of the survivors, 'the tallest and most beautiful were reserved for the Triumph, those under seventeen were sold as slaves, and a great many were sent to the provinces to die in the arenas by the sword and wild beasts.'

But for those who took the Prophetic Word seriously and acted upon it in due time, there was the promise of light and life in the valley of the shadow of death!

Yet another example of prophecy issuing in acts of salvation and deliverance, is found in 2 Chronicles, chapter twenty.

Facing a confederation of hostile enemies, bent on Judah's total destruction, King Jehoshaphat feared and set himself to seek the Lord, proclaiming a fast throughout the land. The people gathered as one man in Jerusalem, to ask help from the Lord.

Midway through the prayer meeting, there was a 'Holy Spirit interruption' – Heaven answered earth with a promise of divine intervention!

'Then the Spirit of the L<small>ORD</small> came upon Jahaziel ... in the midst of the congregation;

And he said, "Listen, all you of Judah and you inhabitants of Jerusalem, and you King Jehoshaphat! Thus says the L<small>ORD</small> to you: 'Do not be afraid nor dismayed because of this great multitude, for the battle is not yours, but God's.

Tomorrow go down against them. They will surely come up by the ascent of Ziz, and you will find them at the end of the brook before the wilderness of Jeruel.

You will not need to fight in this battle. Position yourselves, stand still and see the salvation of the L<small>ORD</small>, who is with you, O Judah and Jerusalem! Do not fear or be dismayed; tomorrow go out against them, for the L<small>ORD</small> is with you.'"'   (2 Chronicles 20:14–17)

Once again, take note of the practical nature of God's instruction. *A time:* tomorrow. *A place:* the end of the brook. *A strategy:* position yourselves, stand still and see.

The phrase, 'stand still,' does not signify passive inactivity; rather, it is a euphemism for praise and worship. It denotes the stance of a servant before his master, that is, one who waits upon the Lord, and the stance of a priest before the altar, that is, one who offers up sacrifices to the Lord.

With this understanding, Jehoshaphat acted upon the word of the Lord and appointed a choir of singers and musicians to form the vanguard of the army. Armed with the high praises of the living God, they marched before the men of war, singing and chanting: *'Praise the L<small>ORD</small>, for His mercy endures forever.'*

As they began to sing and praise, the angels of the Lord went into action and set ambushes against the invading armies, thereby causing them to kill and destroy one another!

The secret of Jehoshaphat and Judah's success can be summarized in three points:

1. In their distress, they sought the Lord with all of their heart.
2. In their seeking after God, they received a prophecy containing clear and concise instructions for prophetic action.
3. In prompt reverence, they acted upon the Word of the Lord, implementing God's revealed agenda without hesitation or qualification.

On the morning of the prophetic action, Jehoshaphat addressed the people with these words of encouragement:

> *'Hear me, O Judah and you inhabitants of Jerusalem: believe in the LORD your God, and you shall be established; believe His prophets, and you shall prosper.'*
> (2 Chronicles 20:20)

Most readers of this book believe in the Lord; no problem! But believing His prophets and His *Prophetic Word* is an altogether different matter!

Smith Wigglesworth, the great Apostle of Faith of the early Twentieth Century, would often exclaim: **'Faith is an act!'**

'Pistis', the Greek word translated 'faith' in the New Testament, denotes *a total commitment of the whole person to God and His Word*. It signifies *heart confidence, mental assent and physical action*. Faith is acting on the Word of God!

To believe the Prophetic Word is to act on the Prophetic Word. And prophetic action that is based on a truly Prophetic Word opens up the windows of heaven for the blessings of the Lord to be poured out in super-abundant measure!

God will surely bless the work of our hands and cause our every endeavour to prosper, when the action we take is in line with the Prophetic Word of the Lord!

Nevertheless at Your Word

Prophetic action, based on the Prophetic Word of the Lord, has high-yield potential. However, such action requires a certain reckless abandon, as demonstrated by the word 'nevertheless'.

Obedience to the Prophetic Word often flies in the face of human cognizance. That is not to say that prophetic action is irrational, but rather, 'super-rational'. Prophetic action is based on knowledge that lies beyond the scope of human perception. Because of the transcendent nature of spiritual truth, such action often appears strange, if not downright ridiculous, to the untrained and undiscerning eye.

As high as the heavens are above the earth, so superior are God's ways to our ways, and God's thoughts to our thoughts (Isaiah 55:9). The Lord Jesus lived and moved in this transcendent realm of the Spirit. Consequently, many of His words and actions went over the top of the disciples' heads. But the bottom line of Jesus' spirituality, was His absolute practicality! It worked!

An example of the transcendence of the Prophetic Word and the corresponding demands that such a word makes upon one's faith, is found in the fifth chapter of the Gospel of Luke.

Simon Peter was a fisherman extraordinaire, an undisputed expert in the business of Galilean trawling. By contrast, Jesus was a professional carpenter – great with hammer and nails, but unskilled and inexperienced in the art of catching fish.

Simon and his crew had apparently been out on the lake all night, toiling with their nets. As the light of dawn broke across the hills of the Golan, they slowly headed back to Capernaum, their nets empty and their spirits low.

Arriving back at port, they secured the boats and proceeded to wash and repair the nets. Before long, a crowd started to gather on the shoreline, and soon, the focus of their attention came into view as Jesus, the great Rabbi from Nazareth, walked along the beach, surrounded by a crush of people.

Much to Simon's surprise, Jesus stepped into his boat and asked him to put out a little from the shore. Simon's boat was thus summarily transformed into a floating pulpit, from which the Lord proclaimed the Gospel of the Kingdom to the multitudes!

When He had concluded His message, Jesus turned to Simon and said, *'Launch out into the deep and let down your nets for a catch.'* Jesus the Carpenter-Rabbi, telling Simon the Arch-Fisherman how to catch fish! Or was it the Spirit of God in Jesus, sharing a fragment of God's transcendent wisdom and knowledge through a word of prophecy!

Simon's response to this challenging and provocative word constitutes a classic case study in prophetic action:

> *'But Simon answered and said to Him, "Master, we have toiled all night and caught nothing; nevertheless at Your Word I will let down the net."*
>
> *And when they had done this, they caught a great number of fish, and their net was breaking.'*

> (Luke 5:5, 6)

'Nevertheless,' in spite of what my five senses tell me, in spite of the dictates of personal experience and professional training, in spite of what others may think or say, *'at your Word.'* You know things that I do not know, You see things that I cannot see, therefore, I will trust Your greater wisdom and knowledge, and act on Your Word.

The result? A net-breaking, boat-sinking load! Superabundance from the hand of God! A miracle-harvest!

In His merciful sovereignty, God allowed Simon to experience the failure of human enterprise, in order to demonstrate the unchanging truth of Zechariah 4:6; *'Not by might nor by power, but by My Spirit, says the LORD of Hosts.'*

Jesus was teaching Simon and his fellow fishermen a kingdom principle that would undergird their future ministry as apostles in the New Testament Church: *'Do not be afraid, from now on you will catch men.'*

In other words, 'The principle you have learned in this

incident will operate in any kind of life situation, including the winning of lost souls to the Lord.' The principle being that *prophetic action, based on the Prophetic Word of the Lord, releases the creative ability of the Holy Spirit to accomplish gre · exploits for the glory of God!*

Sitting Until We Die

Failure to act on the Prophetic Word of the Lord can be enormously costly, both in terms of spiritual blessing and physical well-being. A study in modern Jewish history graphically illustrates this point.

With the Balfour Declaration of November 2nd, 1917, which favoured the establishment of a Jewish homeland in Palestine, and the capture of Jerusalem five weeks later by British troops under the command of General Edmund Allenby, the way was prepared spiritually and politically for the return of the Jewish people from the four corners of the earth, in fulfilment of God's Prophetic Word.

Four hundred years of Ottoman-Moslem domination of the Land had come to an abrupt end, and as touching Jerusalem, without a shot being fired!

General Allenby entered the city on foot, via the Jaffa Gate, with the humility of a pilgrim, not the arrogance of a conqueror. The date was December 11th, the first day of *Chanuka* (the Feast of Lights or Dedication) – a sign to Jews in Jerusalem and around the world that a new day of redemption had dawned.

In 1920, the victorious World War One allies convened a conference in the city of San Remo, on the Italian Riviera. Here, representatives of the great Powers were to sign an agreement for partition of the Middle East. Britain was granted a mandate over Iraq and Palestine, the latter granted with the explicit condition that a Jewish National Homeland be established within it.

Thus, the Balfour Declaration was ratified by an international agreement, which agreement was confirmed by the League of Nations in 1922, and formally declared in effect in 1923.

Another significant event of 1920 was the appointment of Sir Herbert Samuel, a distinguished British Jew, as British High Commissioner to Palestine. For the first time in 1,850 years, a Jew would rule over *Eretz Israel* (the land of Israel).

A most amazing Messianic fervour gripped Jewish Jerusalem with the arrival of Sir Herbert Samuel at the Old City's Hurva Synagogue. Standing in the Bimah for the Torah reading, the High Commissioner came to the famous words: *'Nahamu, Nahamu Ami, Yo'mar Eloheikhem'* (Comfort My people, comfort them, says your God).

In the words of Max Nurock (Secretary to the High Commissioner), the congregation, as it were, shuddered, vibrated, quivered, and from the whole congregation there rose a great sigh, an angel's murmur, to the high heavens and the dome of the Hurva. In that golden moment, the Jews inside the synagogue and all who knew of it outside felt that the hour of redemption had come.

With these events, the gates of Jewish immigration to the Land were thrown wide open. Had they so desired, the Jews could have returned to the Promised Land en masse and might even have established a Jewish State prior to the holocaust of World War Two.

However, the Jewish people's failure to grasp this historic and prophetic opportunity gave rise to Dr Chaim Weizmann's famous appeal, 'Jewish people, where are you?'

Why didn't the Jews respond? There is no easy answer to this vexing question. Of the eight million Jews in Eastern Europe (more than two thirds of World Jewry), and the one million Jews in Western Europe (eight per cent of World Jewry), only a remnant managed to make *Aliyah* before the outbreak of war.

The major obstacle to emigration was undoubtedly the attachment of the Jewish people to their adopted homelands. For some, this attachment represented centuries of family tradition and cultural heritage; for others, it was the security of the known.

Yet again, for some, it was the pleasures of materialism; for others, it was a misplaced patriotism – being 'more German than the Germans'. For many, *Aliyah* (immigration or going up to Zion) meant starting all over again in a desert land – draining the swamps, tilling the ground, building the infrastructure of a new life.

Regrettably, most European Jews considered the price too high and the risk too great. Yet in true Old Testament fashion, *'The LORD God of their fathers sent warnings to them by His messengers, rising up early and sending them, because He had compassion on His people and on His dwelling place'* (2 Chronicles 36:15).

But all too often, *'They mocked the messengers of God, despised His words, and scoffed at His prophets, until the wrath of the LORD arose against His people, till there was no remedy'* (2 Chronicles 36:16).

Therefore, *'He brought against them the king of the Chaldeans, who killed their young men with the sword in the house of their sanctuary, and had no compassion on young man or virgin, on the aged or the weak; He gave them all into his hand'* (2 Chronicles 36:17).

In this case, the 'messengers of the Lord' were the Zionists; the *'king of the Chaldeans'* was Adolf Hitler and his demonically inspired Nazi movement; the slaughter of the Jewish people was the holocaust – hell's final solution – in which six million men, women and children perished, simply because they were Jews.

Zionist activists like Ze'ev Jabotinsky travelled through Europe in the 1920s and 30s, urging and even pleading with the Jews to take prophetic action: *'Get out while you can; go to Palestine and resettle the Land; things are not going to get better in Europe, only worse; the ground is burning under your feet!'*

The tragedy of inertia in the face of divine opportunity is nowhere more clearly seen than in this terrible page of Jewish history. Christians would do well to learn a lesson from God's ancient Covenant people, for the blessings and judgments of God are to the Jew first, and then to the Gentile (Romans 2:9, 10).

May the cry of the four lepers at the Gate of Samaria echo in our hearts: *'Why are we sitting here until we die?'* (2 Kings 7:3).

The cost of obeying the Prophetic Word is negligible in comparison to the cost of disobedience. To sit idly by when God has spoken is to court trouble and adversity. When the Early Church grew comfortable in Jerusalem and failed to act on the command to evangelize the world, the Lord raised up a great persecution to *'encourage'* them to go! (Acts 8)

Shortly after His resurrection, the Lord Jesus appeared to the eleven disciples as they sat at the table. They were not doing anything bad; they were just not doing anything at all! Jesus proceeded to rebuke their unbelief and hardness of heart (evidenced by their inactivity), because they did not believe the report of His resurrection (Mark 16:14).

What Jesus said to the eleven then, He also says to us today:

'Go ... act on My word ... and I will be with you!'

Chapter 9

Prophesying with Signs and Wonders

The Prophetic Word is a *visible word*; something that can be seen, recognized and understood by the community of God's people. The Lord said to the prophet Habakkuk:

> *'Write the vision, and engrave it so plainly upon tablets that every one who passes may be able to read (it easily and quickly) as he hastens by.'*
>
> (Habakkuk 2:2, Amplified)

Moreover, the Prophetic Word is very often a *demonstrative word*; something that is modelled by God-given signs and wonders.

In Pentecostal and Charismatic circles, there is a standard delivery system or traditional *modus operandi* for the Gifts of the Spirit. Traditions are not necessarily wrong, but they can be very limiting. In the event of a new movement of God, traditional form and interpretation can become the enemy of spiritual progress.

In a truly Spirit-filled church, it is not unusual for a man or a woman to stand up and speak by inspiration of the Holy Spirit. It may be a message in a language of the Spirit, accompanied by an interpretation in the native tongue, or a prophetic utterance in the native tongue.

However, prophetic utterance that is according to the pattern of both Old and New Testaments, is frequently accompanied by demonstrative action – signs and wonders, given by God to model the spoken word.

Consider the following example from Acts chapter twenty-one. The Apostle Paul was sailing down the Mediterranean coast before heading inland to Jerusalem. Passing through Tyre and Ptolemais, the ship finally docked at the port of Caesarea, where Paul and his companions took their leave.

Living in Caesarea was a man by the name of Philip, a mighty evangelist and one of the original seven deacons in the church at Jerusalem. This man was blessed of God with a household of faith – four virgin daughters who flowed in the gift of prophecy!

During the course of Paul's stay with Philip and his family, a prophet came down to visit them from Judea, Agabus by name. And boy, did he stir things up!

> *'When he had come to us, he took Paul's belt, bound his own hands and feet, and said, "Thus says the Holy Spirit, 'So shall the Jews at Jerusalem bind the man who owns the belt, and deliver him into the hands of the Gentiles.'"*
> *And when we heard these things, both we and those from that place pleaded with him not to go up to Jerusalem.'*   (Acts 21:11, 12)

The words and actions of ths man were as one, *together* constituting the prophecy of the Spirit and the revelation of the mind of God.

His *sayings* were modelled by his *signs*: his *words* were confirmed by his *works*. The actions of the prophet spoke volumes, thereby complementing the Word of the Lord that was in his mouth.

Prophetic Lifestyles

It is gloriously possible to so come under the influence of the Holy Spirit that one's conduct becomes prophetic.

One's speech and one's behaviour should be equally anointed of God to form, as it were, a joint testimony of truth.

One can so walk in the Spirit that one's lifestyle, albeit consciously or unconsciously, becomes a sign and a wonder from the hand of the Lord – a supernatural demonstration of the Spirit that captures the attention of the people, awakens them to spiritual issues and instils in them the reverential fear of almighty God.

The Hebrew word '*owth*', translated 'sign', denotes a *prophetic signal, omen, token, or warning*. It also contains the idea of *demonstrative evidence, or visible proof*.

'*Mopheth*', the Hebrew word translated 'wonder', denotes a *prodigy, miracle, marvel and portent*. It is derived from the word '*yapha*', meaning *bright and beautiful*.

By virtue of its miraculous nature, a wonder is highly conspicuous. In fact, it draws people like bees to honey and moths to a flame!

> '*Here am I and the children whom the LORD has given me! We are for signs and wonders in Israel from the LORD of Hosts, who dwells in Mount Zion.*'
>
> (Isaiah 8:18)

The immediate and historical fulfilment of this scripture is contained in the family of Isaiah. Called as a prophet of the Lord and married to a prophetess, it was almost inevitable that Isaiah should raise 'prophetic children'.

The names that Isaiah conferred upon his sons, *Shear-Jashub* (A remnant shall return) and *Maher-Shalal-Hash-Baz* (Speed the spoil, hasten the booty), together with his own name (Salvation is of the Lord), signified the plans and purposes of God for His people, Israel.

Even the dress of the prophet conveyed a significant message. Isaiah 20:2 indicates that God's servant normally wore a garment of hair-cloth or sackcloth. Hairy sackcloth is used in the Bible as a symbol of repentance. Thus, Isaiah's costume, like that of other notable prophets, was a *sermo propheticus realis*, a prophetic preaching by fact. Before he even opened his mouth, his demeanour proclaimed, 'Repent!'

Like their New Testament counterparts, the Old Testament prophets were commanded by God to model the Prophetic Word with God-given signs and wonders.

> *'At the same time the LORD spoke by Isaiah the son of Amoz, saying, "Go, and remove the sackcloth from your body, and take your sandals off your feet." And he did so, walking naked and barefoot.*
>
> *Then the LORD said, "Just as My servant Isaiah has walked naked and barefoot three years for a sign and a wonder against Egypt and Ethiopia,*
>
> *So shall the King of Assyria lead away the Egyptians as prisoners and the Ethiopians as captives, young and old, naked and barefoot, with their buttocks uncovered, to the shame of Egypt."'* (Isaiah 20:2–4)

Take special note of the phrase, *'Just as'*. The Prophetic Word is often accompanied by *just as* signs. They are God's 'special effects', designed to draw attention to and place particular emphasis on His word.

In like manner, the Lord instructed Ezekiel to lay on his left side for three hundred and ninety days, a day for each year, to signify the appointed punishment for Israel's iniquity. Upon completion of the course, he was to turn on his right side and lay in that position for a further forty days, to signify the punishment meted out to Judah.

This symbolic action was consummated by a strong Prophetic Word concerning the siege of Jerusalem. At the same time, Ezekiel was instructed to take a clay tablet and portray on it a city, Jerusalem:

> *'And now, Son of dust, take a large brick and lay it before you and draw a map of the city of Jerusalem on it.*

Draw a picture of siege mounds being built against the city, and enemy camps around it, and battering rams surrounding the walls.

And put an iron plate between you and the city, like a wall of iron. Demonstrate how an enemy army will capture Jerusalem!' (Ezekiel 4:1–3, TLB)

This action may be termed, 'Prophetic art'. The expression of the mind of God in enduring art form, as a witness to a nation and a generation.

The Spoken Word is the primary means of prophesying or expressing the mind of God, however, it is not the exclusive means by which spiritual truth is conveyed. Almighty God can speak prophetically via the printed page, music, drama and graphic art. We should not limit the creative expression of the Spirit of God by our narrow-based experience.

The Lord then said something very profound to Ezekiel, something that will change your life, if you let it penetrate your spirit:

'There is special meaning in each detail of what I have told you to do. For it is a warning to the people of Israel.' (Ezekiel 4:3, TLB)

What an encouragement to walk in the Spirit and obey the Lord! There is *special meaning* in *every detail* of what God tells us to do!

Though we may not see it at the time, though we may not understand its significance, *there is special meaning in God's instructions!* If we act in faith, we will surely see the Glory of God!

For this reason, the Apostle Paul exhorted Christians to be strong and steady, always doing what God tells them to do, knowing that nothing they do for the Lord is ever wasted – nothing in God is without effect or significance! (1 Corinthians 15:58)

Yet another example of the working relationship

between prophetic signs and prophetic proclamation can be found in the book of Jeremiah, chapter nineteen:

> *'Thus says the LORD: "Go and get a potter's earthen flask, and take some of the elders of the people and some of the elders of the priests.*
>
> *And go out to the valley of the Son of Hinnom, which is by the entry of the Potsherd Gate; and proclaim there the Word that I will tell you...*
>
> *Then you shall break the flask in the sight of the men who are with you,*
>
> *And say to them, 'Thus says the LORD of Hosts: "Even so I will break this people and this city, as one breaks a potter's vessel, which cannot be made whole again; and they shall bury them in Tophet till there is no place to bury."'"'*
>
> (Jeremiah 19:1–2, 10–11)

Once again, it is the phrase *'even so'*, or *'just as'*, that connects action with utterance. *'Just as I have signified by the action of My servant,'* says the Lord, *'even so will I do by the power of My Spirit.'*

And so we could go on, drawing upon scriptural example after scriptural example, and highlighting prophetic incident after prophetic incident. Suffice to say that, upon the sheer weight of biblical evidence, signs and wonders are effective and indispensable tools of prophetic communication!

Demonstrations of the Spirit

The preaching of the Apostle Paul was consistently punctuated by divine manifestations of power, that not only confirmed the validity of the message and the authenticity of the messenger, but also illustrated the substance of the word.

> *'For I will not dare to speak of any of those things which Christ has not accomplished through me, in word and deed, to make the Gentiles obedient –*

> *In mighty signs and wonders, by the power of the*
> *Spirit of God, so that from Jerusalem and round about*
> *to Illyricum I have fully preached the Gospel of Christ.'*
> (Romans 15:18, 19)

Like other men of God in the Bible, Paul makes the
connection between 'word and deed' or 'speech and
action', that action being 'mighty signs and wonders performed in the power of the Spirit of God'.

According to Paul, the joint testimony of word and deed
constitutes a *complete presentation* of the gospel of Messiah: 'In this way, I have fully preached the gospel.'

Writing to the Church at Corinth, Paul recounted his
earlier visit to the bustling metropolis:

> *'And I, brethren, when I came to you, did not come*
> *with excellence of speech or of wisdom declaring to you*
> *the testimony of God...*
> *And my speech and my preaching were not with*
> *persuasive words of human wisdom, but in demonstra-*
> *tion of the Spirit and of power, that your faith should*
> *not be in the wisdom of men but in the power of God.'*
> (1 Corinthians 2:1, 4, 5)

The testimony of God can only truly be declared in words
that the Holy Spirit teaches; spiritual things must be
expounded with spiritual words. In this sense, all preaching, teaching, praying, praising and witnessing should be
prophetic – empowered and directed by the Holy Spirit.

Coming to the bastion of hedonism that was Corinth,
Paul determined not to speak of anything except Jesus the
Messiah and His work on the Cross. He did not seek to
sway the people with subtle arguments or persuade them
with human philosophy. Instead, he cast himself entirely
upon the person of the Holy Spirit and the operation of His
power.

In spite of Paul's natural weakness, fear and trembling,
his message and proclamation were attended by supernatural manifestations of the presence of God. The Holy

Spirit moved in remarkable demonstrations of power. Signs and wonders accompanied the preaching of the Word.

The point of this real-life example is that whenever the message of God is proclaimed, *prophetically*, there will be demonstrations of the Spirit to confirm and model the Word.

The net result of speaking and acting by the Spirit is the edification of the Church in faith and love: *'That your faith should not be in the wisdom of men but in the power of God.'*

Prophesy – with signs and wonders – for a release of faith in the power of God!

Chapter 10

Prophesying by Weight and Measure

'A false balance is an abomination to the Lord,' declared King Solomon, *'but a just weight is His delight'* (Proverbs 11:1). Furthermore, *'All the weights in the bag are His concern'* (Proverbs 16:11). Indeed, all things are naked and open to the eyes of Him to Whom we must give account. There is absolutely nothing hidden from His sight, not even the thoughts and intents of the heart!

Accurate scales and honest measurements are fundamental conditions for perpetuity of life and ministry. The Lord said to Israel:

> *'You shall not have in your bag different weights, a heavy and a light.*
> *You shall not have in your house different measures, a large and a small.*
> *You shall have a perfect and just weight, a perfect and just measure, that your days may be lengthened in the land which the LORD your God is giving you.'*
>
> (Deuteronomy 25:13–15)

Spiritual gifts, including the ministries of tongues and interpretation and prophetic utterance, are to be judged and regulated according to certain immutable weights and measures – those weights and measures being the apostolic principles of the New Testament.

In concluding his masterful dissertation on the Gifts of the Spirit, the Apostle Paul declared:

> *'Let all things be done decently and in order.'*
> (1 Corinthians 14:40)

'Let all things be done.' What things? To find the answer, one must examine the context of Paul's statement. The Apostle has just spent several chapters talking about the multi-membered Body of Christ with its manifold gifts and ministries.

Clearly, *'all things'* has to do with the Gifts of the Holy Spirit; *'Be done'* refers to their operation in the local church. *Let the Gifts of the Spirit be employed in the church decently and in order!*

The Greek word *'euschemonos'*, translated 'decently', is a compilation of two words, *'eu'* and *'schema'*, meaning *well-formed*. *'Euschemonos'* denotes *decorum and deportment, propriety and nobility; speaking and acting gracefully, becomingly, honestly, honourably, and in a seemly manner.*

'Taxis', the Greek word translated 'order', is a derivative of *'tasso'*, *to arrange in an orderly manner*. It speaks of a *due order*, or a *standard rule of procedure*.

There is a due order of service and a standard rule of procedure in the House of God, to which all gifts and ministries must conform. This 'due order' and 'standard rule' is set down in the Word of God, which is forever settled in Heaven.

> *'...I write so that you may know how you ought to conduct yourself in the House of God, which is the Church of the Living God, the pillar and ground of the Truth.'*
> (1 Timothy 3:15)

The culture of the Kingdom of God transcends ethnic culture, parochial tradition, personal preference and present convenience. Heaven's propriety is based upon the righteousness and holiness of God, which is both timeless and universal. It is equally applicable to all peoples in all nations throughout all generations!

The written word of the holy Scripture is the 'plumb-line' that God has set in the midst of His Church, according to which all gifs and ministries, including prophecy, must be measured and judged. (Amos 7:7, 8)

Let us now consider those weights and measures that pertain to the ministry of prophetic utterance in the New Testament Church:

Prophecy Must Meet the Criterion of Biblical Revelation

In the words of the Apostle Paul, *'All Scripture is given by inspiration of God* (literally, is *God-breathed*), *and is profitable for doctrine, for reproof, for correction, for instruction in righteousness, that the man of God may be complete, thoroughly equipped for every good work'* (2 Timothy 3:16, 17).

The philosophies of men are like grass that withers and flowers that fade, but the Word of our God stands forever – immutable, eternal and absolute (Isaiah 40:8).

The written Word is the benchmark of truth and the litmus test of all purported prophetic revelation. The Spirit of God authored the written Word; therefore, He always speaks in unanimity with the record of Scripture.

When a prophetic utterance is delivered, the first question that should be asked is, *'Does the substance and spirit of this prophecy concur with the Word of God?'*

It would behove us to become like the Jews of Berea who *'received the Word with all readiness'* (without scepticism or cynicism), but at the same time *'searched the Scriptures daily to find out whether these things were so'* (Acts 17:11).

May God also help us to remember the admonition of Paul in Galatians 1:8; *'But even if we, or an angel from Heaven, preach any other Gospel to you than what we have preached to you, let him be accursed.'*

Prophecy Must Be the Truth Spoken in Love

The Apostle Paul shared the secret of spiritual growth in his letter to the Church at Ephesus: *'But, speaking the truth in love, may grow up in all things into Him who is the Head – Christ'* (Ephesians 4:15).

New Testament prophecy is the truth of God, spoken in a spirit of love. As we have noted, prophecy is the expression of God's heart, as well as being the declaration of His mind.

For this reason, true prophecy is utterly incapable of being cold and clinical or dispassionate and detached. If prophecy is the reaching out of the Spirit of God to one of His children, then it must of necessity become passionately involved with the object of ministry.

Prophecy must be conceived and delivered in love. Even when the Spirit of God speaks the truth of correction and discipline, it is spoken in love, with a view to redemption.

To those who call the fire of judgment and condemnation down from Heaven in their prophecies, the Lord Jesus would say: *'You do not know what manner of spirit you are of'* (Luke 9:55).

It is no accident that the Apostle Paul's teaching on the operation of spiritual gifts in First Corinthians is 'interrupted' by a magnificent ode to *agape love* – the unconditional and sacrificial love of God.

Paul clearly shows that prophecy, like all spiritual gifts, should be motivated by love, with a view to the building up of the Body of Messiah for the glory of God! Anything less is sub-normal and unacceptable.

Healthy prophecy issues from a consummate love for the Lord Jesus and His Body, the Church. Love is the wellspring and conduit of spiritual power. Like a protective sheath around an electrical current, love makes the transmission of spiritual gifts safe and profitable.

The imperative of *agape love* is elucidated by the Apostle in 1 Corinthians 13:2; *'Though I have the gift of prophecy, and understand all mysteries and all knowledge, and though*

I have all faith, so that I could remove mountains, but have not love, I am nothing.'

Continuing this theme in chapter fourteen, Paul says: *'Pursue love, and desire spiritual gifts, but especially that you may prophesy.' Love*, and *spiritual gifts*, in that order!

In a spirit of love, prophetic gifts will be properly employed and prophetic revelation will be properly administered for the common good of all.

Love first, and *prophecy* second; that's a safe combination!

Prophecy Must Be Judged By Mature Believers

All prophecy should be judged, regardless of whether it is delivered by a well-known prophet, a scholarly Bible teacher, or a newly-saved believer.

The Apostle Paul laid down this ground-rule in 1 Corinthians 14:29: *'Let two or three prophets speak, and let the others judge.'*

The Greek word '*diakrino*', translated 'judge', means to *separate thoroughly, discriminate and discern*. Edgar Goodspeed translates it this way: *'. . . while the rest weigh what is said.'*

Once again, let us point out that the scale on which prophecy is to be weighed is the unchanging standard of God's written word and the certain witness of the Holy Spirit.

Prophecy should be neither accepted or rejected on the basis of personal preference. God's word and God's Spirit are the only truly righteous and independent arbiters in cases of discriminatory judgment.

It is also important to distinguish between *discriminatory judgment* and doubtful criticism or cynical scepticism. Jesus said, *'Judge not, that you be not judged'* (Matthew 7:1). In other words, 'Don't be critical or cynical. Don't set yourself up as a judge of your brother. Don't be a sheriff in the Kingdom.'

Yet, on the other hand, the Apostle Paul admonished: *'Test all things; hold fast what is good'* (1 Thessalonians 5:21). To put it another way, 'Discern the spiritual quality and moral value of all things, with a view to approving that which is true and good.'

Paul warns against adopting a cynical attitude toward prophecy in 1 Thessalonians 5:20: *'Do not despise prophecies.'* The Greek word *'exoutheneo'*, translated 'despise', means to *make of no account, regard as nothing*, and *treat with contempt.*

Low esteem of spiritual gifts is in reality, low esteem of the Holy Spirit, for His gifts are manifestations of His presence and power in the Church. One must be careful not to make light of the prophetic ministry, for in doing so one can grieve and offend the Spirit and quench the flow of His inspiration.

Yet, we do have a mandate to examine every prophetic utterance with spiritual sensitivity, in deference to the final authority of God's written Word. The Expositor's Greek Testament states succinctly:

> 'In applying the standard of spiritual discernment, it must sift, not for the mere pleasure of rejecting the erroneous but with the object of retaining what is genuine.'   (Volume 4, page 42)

I have no problem with personal prophecy that is delivered in a public gathering such as the local church and is thereby open to the judgment of mature spiritual believers. But I do have a problem with personal prophecy that is delivered in a corner, away from the public eye, with no independent witnesses as judges.

Every occurrence of personal prophecy in the New Testament is recorded in the context of plural witnesses. The previously quoted prophecy of Agabus over the Apostle Paul, in Philip's house at Caesarea, is one such example.

There may be occasions when it is logistically impossible to summon the attendance of other believers to hear the word of the Lord. However, this should be the rare exception and not the general rule.

I cannot help but be deeply suspicious of people who refuse to submit their prophetic utterances to the objective scrutiny of fellow believers. If the word is of God, it will stand the test of healthful examination.

May God's Word be the last word on the subject: *'Let two or three prophesy, and let the others judge.'*

Prophecy Must Be Delivered in the Humility of Messiah

'We know in part and we prophesy in part' (1 Corinthians 13:9). Remembering this fact will help keep you humble whenever God uses you as his 'telegraph boy'.

The whole tenor of Paul's teaching on the gift of prophecy in 1 Corinthians 14 is one of humility and servanthood.

'But if anything is revealed to another who sits by, let the first keep silent.' The Spirit of Messiah is a spirit of deference, in honour preferring one another, regarding others as more important than oneself (Romans 12:10; Philippians 2:3).

'The spirits of the prophets are subject to the prophets.' The hallmark of true anointing is self-control, as against impetuosity, which is a sign of the flesh (2 Timothy 1:7).

W.J. Conybeare, in *The Epistles of Paul*, translates it this way: 'The gift of prophecy does not take away from the prophets the control of their own spirits.'

Holy Spirit inspiration is not a license for zany behaviour. No one should lose control and then piously exclaim, 'The Holy Spirit led me to do it.' According to Romans 8:13–14, the leading of the Spirit issues in the putting to death of the unfruitful works of the flesh.

The Spirit does not lead us to show off our prowess for the purpose of personal gain and glory. Rather, He leads us to serve the Body in the Prophetic Word with the humility that characterizes the person and work of Messiah Jesus!

Recognize Those Who Labour Among You

To the Church at Thessalonica, Paul said: *'We urge you, brethren, to recognize those who labour among you, and are over you in the Lord and admonish you'* (1 Thessalonians 5:12).

The Greek word *'oida'*, translated 'recognize', signifies to *see* or *perceive*, and hence, to *know from observation*. The word carries the connotation of respect and appreciation for the virtuous character and diligent service of an individual over an extended period of observation.

Admittedly, the context of Paul's exhortation reveals that he is talking about respect for elders who have proved themselves worthy leaders of God's flock.

However, by extension of biblical principle, this rule can also be rightfully applied to any person who exercises a spiritual gift or ministry in the local church.

Those who are qualified to minister are those who are 'known' or 'recognized', not just as regular attendants or long-standing members, but as Godly men and women of virtuous character and blameless behaviour.

The clear implication of First Corinthians chapter fourteen is that those who exercise spiritual gifts in the congregation are not strangers, but recognized *and approved* members.

There is much to be said for testing a person's character through a period of close observation before allowing them to minister in a public capacity.

The Apostolic rule of 'Proving and Approving' is clearly set forth in first Timothy chapter three and Titus chapter one for all who aspire to the office of a deacon or an elder.

It would be a healthy safeguard to apply a similar standard of qualification to all gifts and ministries, especially to the vocal gifts of tongues, interpretation and prophecy.

In the final analysis, a man will prophesy out of the abundance of his heart. It would behove us therefore, to recognize or know through observation the character of those who speak prophetically in our midst.

Chapter 11

Prophesying ... Some Practical Steps

Like all other spiritual gifts, prophecy remains the exclusive property of the Holy Spirit. Although we may be used to manifest the gift, we cannot claim to 'have' the gift as though it is a personal possession, to use whenever, wherever, and however we choose.

When handling the gifts of the Spirit, we must tread with godly reverence, so as not to infringe upon the sovereign propriety of the Spirit, who is the gift-giver. Remember that in handling God's gifts, we are actually handling tangible expressions of His glory!

We cannot prophesy when we like, how we like and to whom we like. Prophecy is the province of the Holy Spirit, and as such, is regulated according to His will. In the words of Paul, '*One and the same Spirit works all these things, distributing to each one individually* **as He wills**' (1 Corinthians 12:11).

However, in sounding that cautionary note, let us also remember that God is much more desirous of speaking to us than we are of hearing Him, and moreover, much more desirous of speaking *through* us than we are of being His mouthpiece!

Jesus said that the Spirit would speak to us whatever He hears from the Father and the Son (John 16:13). One thing is certain: the Spirit has not stopped speaking! There is no diminishing of the prophetic flow from God's throne!

Therefore, having settled the issue of God's sovereignty

over His gifts, let us also consider the matter of man's responsibility to prepare himself as a vessel for the manifestation of the Spirit.

> *'But in a great house there are not only vessels of gold and silver, but also of wood and clay, some for honour and some for dishonour.*
>
> *Therefore if anyone cleanses himself from the latter, he will be a vessel for honour, sanctified and useful for the Master, prepared for every good work.'*
>
> (2 Timothy 2:20, 21)

The operation of the gift of prophecy is determined by the will of the Master, yet, at the same time, is dependent on the readiness of the servant.

May it never be said of us: *'I sought for a man among them who would stand before Me and hear My voice, and take My word to his generation, but I found none!'*

No! When the Lord gives the word, let there be a great company of prophets ready to proclaim it, in Jesus' Name!

Following are four guide-lines of preparation for spiritual usefulness in the House of the Lord:

1. Pray in the Spirit

Speaking in spiritual languages (tongues) is the getting on point for service in the Gifts of the Spirit.

Praying in the Spirit sensitizes one to the realm of God's gifts and callings. Indeed, *glossolalia* plugs one into the mind of God and makes one receptive to His thoughts and desires in any given area!

Thus, praying in the Spirit paves the way for prophetic revelation. Quite obviously, the more we speak in tongues, the more useful we become to the Holy Spirit ... the more sensitive to His will in the face of human need ... and the more responsive to His manifestation in each and every situation!

If you desire to be used of God in prophecy, cultivate a

relationship of intimacy with Him through the languages of the Spirit!

2. Let the Word Dwell in You Richly

Out of the abundance of the heart the mouth speaks, and when the heart is full of the Word of God, that is precisely what flows forth under the anointing of the Holy Spirit.

A sound prophecy will always have a high 'Word content', for the Word is the inscribed mind and will of God unto all generations.

In Apostolic Christianity, the prerequisite to public ministry was a Christlike character, an anointing of the Spirit, and a knowledge of the Word: *'Seek out from among you seven men of good reputation, full of the Holy Spirit and wisdom, whom we may appoint over this business ... and they chose Stephen, a man full of faith and the Holy Spirit'* (Acts 6:3, 5).

In the same vein, the Apostle Paul admonished the Colossian Christians to *'let the Word of God dwell in their hearts richly in all wisdom,'* so that they would be equipped to *'teach and admonish one another in psalms and hymns and spiritual songs, and to sing with grace in their hearts to the Lord'* (Colossians 3:16).

3. Forsake Not the Assembling of Yourselves Together

No man lives unto himself, and no man can make it on his own. The One who in the beginning said, *'It is not good for man to be alone,'* is the same One who sets solitary believers in spiritual families.

You need to be part of a local church where the whole counsel of God is proclaimed, where the presence and power of God is in consistent manifestation, and where the gifts of the Spirit are in regular operation.

Local churches such as this are healthy breeding grounds for New Testament gifts and ministries. They provide an example to follow, an encouragement to persevere, and a protective check and balance for a successful ministry in the Spirit.

4. Consecrate a Fast

Fasting is a spiritual discipline, issuing in the subjugation of the flesh (the carnal nature) and the exaltation of the spirit (the nature of Messiah).

The Book of Joel exhorts us to *'consecrate a fast, call a sacred assembly, gather the elders and all the inhabitants of the land into the House of the LORD our God, and cry out to the LORD'* (Joel 1:14).

Moreover, the Lord calls us to *'turn to Him with all our heart, with fasting, weeping and mourning, and to rend our hearts rather than our garments'* (Joel 2:12, 13).

The sacred assembly of which Joel speaks, is a national convocation of prayer and fasting, as an expression of humility and repentance before the Lord.

As a result, the Lord will be zealous for His land and pity His people; He will answer them from heaven with a plentiful rain and an abundance of new wine and oil (symbols of a spiritual outpouring of grace and power).

Then comes this wonderful promise of the Holy Spirit, upon which so much of our theological practice is based: *'And it shall come to pass afterward that I will pour out My Spirit on all flesh; your sons and daughters shall prophesy, your old men shall dream dreams, your young men shall see visions'* (Joel 2:28).

'Afterward.' After what? After a holy convocation of prayer and fasting that brings forth real repentance and reverence in the lives of God's people!

The lesson is simple: corporate prayer and fasting precipitates new outpourings of the Holy Spirit and new demonstrations of His grace and power in the congregation, in the form of prophecy, dreams, visions, signs and wonders!

The ministry of the Church at Antioch was patterned on

the prophecy of Joel. As the elders of the Church worshipped God with fasting and prayers, the Holy Spirit spoke prophetically: *'Now separate to me Barnabas and Saul for the work to which I have called them'* (Acts 13:1, 2).

Corporate gatherings of praise and worship, holy convocations of prayer and fasting, and sacred assemblies of intercession and supplication, were a way of life in this First Century church for both sheep and shepherds.

The fact remains: Prophecy is the fruit of communion with God, personally and as a congregation. There is no other way!

Chapter 12

Yet for This Will I Be Entreated

How should one respond to a Prophetic Word, given by the Holy Spirit through one of His approved servants?

This question stimulated a desire in my heart to know God and discover the secret of answered prayer and fulfilled prophecy.

Growing up in the Pentecostal church, I witnessed numerous presbytery sessions in which marvellous prophecies were given over Bible College graduates, young pastors, prospective missionaries and would-be evangelists.

However, over the years I became alarmed at the amount of unfulfilled prophecy in the Body of Christ, laying around like furniture at a garage sale. In most cases, the prophecies were scriptural and accurate, yet some were only partially fulfilled and others were not fulfilled at all.

After searching the Scriptures I came to see that while every Word of God contains within itself the power for fulfilment (Luke 1:37), there must be a corresponding response of faith on the part of the recipient of the Word.

In other words, fulfilment of prophecy is not automatic and should never be taken for granted, without appropriate human responsibility.

Is Prophecy Binding?

A thorough investigation of the Word of God reveals that vocal prophecy, as distinct from the canon of Holy

Scripture, is not necessarily binding. In other words, God can change His mind, not whimsically and impetuously, but if human behaviour warrants it.

God gave Jeremiah a lesson in the pivot of the Prophetic Word, when he visited the potter's workshop:

> *'Then I went down to the potter's house, and there he was, making something at the wheel.*
>
> *And the vessel that he made of clay was marred in the hand of the potter; so he made it again into another vessel, as it seemed good to the potter to make.*
>
> *Then the word of the LORD came to me, saying: "O house of Israel, can I not do with you as this potter?" says the LORD. "Look, as the clay is in the potter's hand, so are you in My hand, O house of Israel!*
>
> *"The instant I speak concerning a nation and concerning a kingdom, to pluck up, to pull down, and to destroy it,*
>
> *"if that nation against whom I have spoken turns from its evil, I will relent of the disaster that I thought to bring upon it.*
>
> *"And the instant I speak concerning a nation and concerning a kingdom, to build and to plant it,*
>
> *"if it does evil in My sight so that it does not obey My voice, then I will relent concerning the good with which I said I would benefit it."'* (Jeremiah 18:3–10)

An individual or a nation can abrogate a prophetic promise of blessing and forfeit an inheritance of prosperity through obdurate disobedience. Consider the following illustration from a typical family situation:

Before leaving for work, father kisses his children and says to them, 'How would you like to go to Pizza Hut for dinner?' With squeals of delight, they respond, 'We'd love to!' But when father returns home later in the day, he discovers that his children have thoroughly misbehaved and reduced their mother to tears.

In a stern disciplinarian tone, father says, 'You have

disqualified yourselves from being treated for dinner; no going out, no Pizza Hut!' With wails of anguish they cry, 'But father, you said...'

Whilst father's promise of dinner at the Pizza Hut did not carry any explicit conditions of good behaviour, it was laden with implicit expectations of obedience and responsibility.

And so it is with many of God's promises. They may not have explicit conditions attached to their fulfilment, but they are surely bound by implicit expectations of righteousness.

Likewise, an individual or a nation may avert certain judgment and disaster, though it be prophesied in thunderous tones, through genuine repentance and righteous reform.

The ministry of Jonah in the great and wicked city of Nineveh is one such example. When Jonah finally decided (after strong encouragement!) to obey the Lord and go to Nineveh, he had but one message on his heart: *'Yet forty days and Nineveh shall be overthrown!'* (Jonah 3:4).

There appears to be no window of hope in such a word; no mercy, not even an opportunity to repent! And yet, *'when God saw their works, that they turned from their evil way, He relented from the disaster that He had said He would bring upon them, and He did not do it'* (Jonah 3:10).

On another occasion, the prophet Isaiah went to King Hezekiah and said to him, *'Thus says the LORD: "Set your house in order, for you shall die and not live."'* A rather direct and emphatic word, with no apparent room for negotiation! But Hezekiah turned his face to the wall and poured out his heart unto God.

And it happened, before Isaiah had gone out into the middle court, that the word of the Lord came to him, saying: *'Return and tell Hezekiah the leader of My people, "Thus says the LORD, the God of David your father; I have heard your prayer, I have seen your tears; surely I will heal you. On the third day you shall go up to the house of the LORD. And I will add to your days fifteen years."'* (2 Kings 20:1–6).

117

The gift of prophecy is not eternally binding. God can change His mind, for good or evil, in accordance with a change in human attitude and behaviour.

Inquiring of the Lord

In the thirty-sixth chapter of Ezekiel, the Lord God gives a series of wonderful promises of restoration and inheritance to His wayward people, Israel. Twenty times God says, 'I will, I will, I will!' Yet, the key to this chapter and indeed, to all God's redemptive provision is found in verse thirty-seven:

> *'Thus says the LORD God: "I will also let the house of Israel inquire of Me to do this for them: I will increase their men like a flock."'*

The Hebrew word *'darash'*, translated 'inquire', means to *follow in pursuit or in search of*, to *seek with care*, and by implication, to *ask*. It also contains the idea of *worship*.

God says, *'For the fulfilment of these promises I will be pursued, sought out, asked and worshipped.'*

A similar theme is developed in the book of Isaiah, chapter sixty-two, where God gives another series of marvellous promises concerning the restoration and glorification of Jerusalem.

Yet, midway through the chapter, God interrupts the flow of prophecy with an astounding invitation:

> *'I have set watchmen on your walls, O Jerusalem; they shall never hold their peace day or night. You who make mention of the LORD, do not keep silent,*
>
> *And give Him no rest till He establishes and till He makes Jerusalem a praise in the earth.'*

(Isaiah 62:6, 7)

Without exaggeration, one could say that the fulfilment of God's end-time purposes for Jerusalem is contingent on the appointment of spiritual watchmen and their faithfulness to *'make mention of the Lord.'*

The Hebrew word *'zachar'*, translated 'make mention', means to *put in remembrance, bring to mind, mention, meditate on, mark down, record, recall and retain in one's thoughts.*

In modern Hebrew, *'zachar'* is the word for a secretary. The above quoted definitions certainly form a comprehensive list of secretarial duties!

God's secretaries are those who hear His voice and receive His prophetic or quickened Word in their hearts, and having received His Word, continue to bring it to His attention, reminding Him of His promise and purpose until such time as it comes to pass.

Herein is portrayed a picture of persistence in prayer, praise and thanksgiving – watchmen who do not hold their peace day or night; who do not keep silent; who give the Lord no rest. On the shoulders of such persevering saints rest the Kingdom purposes of almighty God!

I Will Be Found of You

Finding God and the fulfilment of His Prophetic Word in prayer, is a way of life that the Church must embrace ever more deeply as the end of the age looms on the horizon.

End-time Christians can afford to take a page out of Judah's history – another people in another time, who faced 'Apocalypse Now' in their generation.

Through the prophet Jeremiah, the Lord gave the exiled captives of Judah a promise of eventual redemption and restoration:

> *'For thus says the LORD: After seventy years are completed at Babylon, I will visit you and perform My good Word toward you, and cause you to return to this place.*

*For I know the thoughts that I think toward you, says
the LORD, thoughts of peace and not of evil, to give you
a future and a hope.'* (Jeremiah 29:10, 11)

At first glance, the Prophetic Word appears unconditional and guaranteed of self-fulfilment. The Lord has
even forecast a time-frame of completion. But then He
proceeds to announce the 'trigger' that will set off the chain
reaction of prophetic fulfilment.

*'Then you will call upon Me and go and pray to Me,
and I will listen to you.*

*And you will seek Me and find Me, when you search
for Me with all your heart.*

*I will be found by you, says the LORD, and I will
bring you back from your captivity...'*

(Jeremiah 29:12–14a)

There is a due season of fulfilment for every purpose and
promise of God. At such a time, God searches for a person
or a group of people who will stand before Him in the place
of intercession; people who will stir themselves up to seek
the Lord and persist until they find Him; people who will
search for (Hebrew: *'darash'*), follow after, and closely
pursue Him with all their heart, and thereby, prepare the
way for the performance of His Word.

A case in point is the prophet Daniel. Exiled to Babylon
as a young man; strategically placed in the King's court;
promoted through divine favour and supernatural revelation; uncompromisingly righteous in the midst of a wicked
and perverse generation.

Daniel was a man of prayer and a man of the Word.
During his systematic reading of the Scriptures (the Law
and the Prophets), he made an amazing discovery:

'In the first year of his (Darius') *reign, I, Daniel, understood by the books the number of the years specified by
the Word of the LORD through Jeremiah the prophet,*

that He would accomplish seventy years in the desolations of Jerusalem.' (Daniel 9:2)

Upon checking the calendar, Daniel realized that the divinely appointed expiration of the exilic period was at hand. How did he respond to the Prophetic Word and the revelation of God's timing?

'Then I set my face toward the LORD God to make request by prayer and supplications, with fasting, sackcloth, and ashes.

And I prayed to the LORD my God, and made confession, and said...' (Daniel 9:3, 4a)

To 'set one's face' is a Hebrew euphemism for persistent determination in pursuit of a specific goal. The goal, in this case, was to move God to keep His promise and perform His word concerning Jerusalem and the Jewish remnant in Babylon.

The means of achieving this goal was prayer and supplication, enhanced by fasting and repentance.

Did God honour Daniel's intercession? The answer is unequivocally, 'Yes!' Daniel's prayers and supplications 'lit the fuse', so to speak, and activated the now-ripe purposes of God. History bears testimony to the ensuing fulfilment of prophecy:

'Now in the first year of Cyrus king of Persia, that the Word of the LORD by the mouth of Jeremiah might be fulfilled, the LORD stirred up the spirit of Cyrus king of Persia, so that he made a proclamation throughout all his kingdom, and also put it in writing, saying,

Thus says Cyrus king of Persia: All the kingdoms of the earth the LORD God of heaven has given me. And he has commanded me to build Him a house at Jerusalem which is in Judah. Who is among you of all His people? May the LORD his God be with him, and let him go up!' (2 Chronicles 36:22, 23)

Some people receive the Prophetic Word of the Lord and then sit back with the attitude, 'What will be, will be.' But Daniel shows us that 'what will be, won't be' unless we pray it into manifestation!

Be it Unto Me According to Your Word

Another wonderful example of faith's response to the word of the Lord is found in the story of the immaculate conception of our Lord.

The mighty angel Gabriel was sent from the presence of God to the little town of Nazareth in Northern Israel, to a virgin named Mary. What an astonishing experience for a young woman, who, at this point of time was probably no more than sixteen years old!

Still more astounding was the greeting and message that came from the angel's lips: *'Rejoice, highly favoured one, the Lord is with you; blessed are you among women! Do not be afraid, Mary, for you have found favour with God. And behold, you will conceive in your womb and bring forth a Son, and shall call His name **Jesus**.*

'He will be great, and will be called the Son of the Highest; and the Lord God will give Him the throne of His father David. And He will reign over the house of Jacob forever, and of His Kingdom there will be no end.'

This announcement cast Mary into a mental and emotional dilemma: *'How can this be, since I do not know a man?'*

We now come to one of the pivotal points of history; a make or break moment in the purposes of God:

> *'And the angel answered and said to her, "The Holy Spirit will come upon you, and the power of the Highest will overshadow you; therefore, also, that Holy One who is to be born will be called the Son of God ... For with God nothing will be impossible."*
>
> *Then Mary said, "Behold the maidservant of the*

Lord! Let it be to me according to Your Word." And the angel departed from her.'   (Luke 1:35, 37, 38)

What a marvellous promise of grace and glory! *'The Holy Spirit will come upon you, the power of the Highest will overshadow you ... the Holy One who is to be born will be called the Son of God!'*

How did Mary respond to the word of the Lord? Did she say, 'Well, it sounds good, but I'll wait and see if it really comes to pass.'

No! Rising up in faith, she cried out: *'Let it be to me. Let it be to me. Let it be to me. According to Your Word!'* And when Mary's faith reached out and laid hold of the Prophetic Word, the power of God touched her body and the miracle took place!

Shortly after this remarkable encounter, Mary journeyed south to the hill country of Judah to visit her relative Elizabeth, who was also expecting a miracle child.

As Mary entered the house, the glory of God fell upon herself and Elizabeth, causing the latter to exclaim:

'Blessed are you among women, and blessed is the fruit of your womb ... Blessed is she who believed, for there will be a fulfilment of those things which were told her from the Lord.'   (Luke 1:42, 45)

The fulfilment of God's Prophetic Word was contingent on Mary's response of faith. *'Blessed is she who* **believed**, *for there will be a* **fulfilment**...'

The same holds true for you and I today. Those who are blessed with the fulfilment of prophecy are those who believe. And those who believe are those who put the Lord in remembrance ... and give Him no rest ... until He establishes ... and until He makes ... according to that which was spoken.

May this be the watchword of the Omega Generation upon whom the climax of the ages has come:

LET IT BE TO US ACCORDING TO YOUR WORD!

PROPHESY FOR A RELEASE OF FAITH AMONG THE NATIONS!